Physical Characteristics of the Welsh Springer Spaniel

(from The Kennel Club b

C000082638

Hindquarters: Strong and muscular, wide and fully developed. Hindlegs well boned, hocks well let down, stifles moderately angled, neither turning in nor out.

Tail: Well set on and low, never carried above level of back, customarily docked. Lively in action.

Coat: Straight or flat, silky texture, dense, never wiry or wavy. Curly coat highly undesirable. Forelegs and hindlegs above hocks moderately feathered, ears and tail lightly feathered.

Size: Approximate height: dogs 48 cm (19 ins) at withers; bitches 46 cm (18 ins) at withers.

Colour: Rich red and white only.

Welsh Springer Spaniel

by Haja van Wessem

Contents

Welsh Springer Spaniel

Housebreaking and Training Your Welsh Springer Spaniel... 102

by Charlotte Schwartz
Be informed about the importance of training your Welsh Springer Spaniel from the basics of housebreaking and understanding the development of a young dog to executing obedience commands (sit, stay, down, etc.).

Health Care of Your Welsh Springer Spaniel 133

Discover how to select a proper veterinary surgeon and care for your dog at all stages of life. Topics include vaccination scheduling, skin problems, dealing with external and internal parasites and the medical and behavioural conditions common to the breed.

PUBLISHED IN THE UNITED KINGDOM BY:

INTERPET
PUBLISHING
Vincent Lane, Dorking   Surrey RH4 3YX   England

ISBN 1-903098-58-0

All rights reserved.
No part of this book may be reproduced in any form, by photostat, scanner, microfilm, xerography or any other means, or incorporated into any information retrieval system, electronic or mechanical, without the written permission of the copyright owner.
Copyright © 2000 Animalia, Ltd.
Cover patent pending. Printed in Korea.

PHOTO CREDITS
Photos by Isabelle Français,
with additional photos provided by:

Adrienne Bancker
Norvia Behling
TJ Calhoun
Carolina Biological Society
Doskocil
David Dalton
Isabelle Francais
James Hayden-Yoav
James R Hayden
Helga Horsten
Ria Hörter
Carol Ann Johnson
Gundrun Johnson

Bill Jonas
Alice van Kempen
Dr Dennis Kunkel
Mikki Pet Products
Marinus Nijhoff
Colleen M O'Keefe
Phototake
RBP
Mrs J A R Revill
Jean Claude Revy
J Schotte-Slootweg
Dr Andrew Spielman
Haja van Wessem

Illustrations by Angela Begg

The publisher would like to acknowledge the following owners of dogs featured in this book:
Carl & Fran Bloom, Nora Carlton,
Tiny van Gent-Slootweg, Hammalgårdens Kennel, Ria Hörter, David & Lisa Hubler,
Janet & Tom Ing, Marinus Nijhoff,
Sandra & Richard Rohrbacher, Jürgen Wallat,
Haja van Wessem, Mr S and Mrs H Williams

A member of the spaniel family, which are some of the oldest dogs known to man, the Welsh Springer Spaniel is a distinguished gundog who is as striking as he is talented.

EARLY SPANIEL HISTORY

Legend has it that there were Welsh Springer Spaniels as far back as the 15th century. True or not, a fact is that the whole group of spaniels, to which the Welsh Springer Spaniel belongs, can be considered among the oldest dogs known to man. It is very likely that the spaniel got his name from the country surrounding the Mediterranean where he lived, namely Spain. According to other sources he might have got his name from the Basque word *Espana* or from the several spaniel-like breeds in France that are called *épagneuls*. The name spaniel might also be derived from the French *s'éspargner*, which means to crouch.

Spaniels also travelled to Wales where they were the treasured dogs of King Howell Dha (Howell the Good). The King's love for his spaniels went as far as giving them a special mention in one of the country's laws in AD 94: for the price of one spaniel, one could buy a number of goats, women, slaves or geese! However, in recent years the authenticity of this document has been questioned.

The first mention of a spaniel in English literature comes as

Musketeer o' Matherne was bred in July 1932 by Capt. J Gage-Williams.

AMONG THE OLDEST BREEDS
The Welsh Springer Spaniel can be considered amongst the oldest breeds in history, his origins going as far back as the 16th or possibly even the 15th century.

early as Geoffrey Chaucer (1340-1400) and Gaston de Foix, who died in 1391. In the *Canterbury Tales*, Chaucer refers to the spaniel several times (e.g. 'for as a spaynel she wol on him lepe'), which proves that the spaniel was known in England 600 years ago.

Gaston de Foix mentions the spaniel in his work *Miroir de Phoebus*, or as it is also known, *Livre de Chasse*. Gaston de Foix, a feudal baron who lived in France near the Spanish border, was convinced that Spain was the country of origin of the spaniel. 'Another kind of hound there is, that be called hounds for the hawk, and spaniels, for their kind cometh from Spain, notwith-standing that there are many in other countries. And such hounds have many good customs and evil. Also a fair hound for the hawk should have a great head, a great body, and be of fair hue, white or tawny (i.e. pied, speckled or mottled) for they be fairest and of such hue they be commonly the

Rheidol Queen was born in 1933 and is typical of the breed in England during that period.

best. They go before their master, running and wagging their tail, and raise or start fowl and wild beasts. But their right craft is of the partridge and of the quail. They can also be taught to take partridge and quail with the net and they love to swim.'

Another early reference to Spanyellys occurs in the *Boke of St. Albans* (1486), also named the *Book of Field Sports*, written by Dame Juliana Berners, prioress of Sopwell Nunnery, Hertfordshire. It is obviously a school book and it is assumed that the book was written for the use of King Henry IV's son, Prince Henry, to teach him to read and make him acquainted with the names of the animals and phrases used in venery and field sports. In the

BEFORE THE GUN
In the days before the gun was invented, game was caught not only with snares but also with nets. The dog drove the birds towards the fowlers, who stood ready with their nets, and both dog and bird were caught under the net.

book there is frequent mention of spaniels in the royal household. Thus we read that 'Robin, the King's Majesty's Spaniel Keeper' was paid a certain sum for 'hair cloth to rub the Spaniels with.'

THE FIRST SPRINGERS

We find the first mention of springer spaniels and in particular red and white spaniels in the book *Treatise of Englishe Dogges* (1570) by the famed dog scholar Dr Caius (pseudonym for John Keyes). Dr Caius described the way the dogs were taught to let themselves be caught under the net and classified all sporting dogs under two headings: *Venatici*, used for the purpose of hunting beasts, and *Auscupatorii*, used for the hunting of fowl. He subdivided this latter group into land spaniels and 'Spaniells

Pat of Merrymount was a very prolific and successful sire of many fine Welsh Springers. He was owned by the Reverend D Stewart, who was one of the great promoters of the breed.

which findeth game on the water.' He named this group *Hispaniolus*. He also was of the opinion that these originated in Spain. He refers to 'the spanniells whose skynnes are white, and if they are marked with any spottes, they are commonly red.'

In the days of Henry VIII, the many royal banquets required great amounts of food, particularly game. Game such as partridges,

Three Welsh Springers owned by Mr J S Jones, photographed at their Crufts debut in 1934.

> **'CORRIN'**
> Welsh Springer history begins with Corrin, who was born in 1893 and registered as a Welsh Cocker, but whose offspring formed the basis of the Welsh Springer breed as it is today.

quail and pheasant, rabbits and hares were caught in snares but because of the never-ending demand, a more speedy method of

Scott Langley, the British canine artist, made this sketch entitled 'Welsh Springer Spaniels' in 1931.

catching the game was needed. This method was found in 'netting.' Spaniels were used to drive the birds towards the fowlers who stood ready with their extended nets. Dog and bird were caught under the net. The spaniels that were used for this kind of work were called sitting or setting spaniels, and they are the ancestors of our modern setters.

With the invention of the gun, netting disappeared and game was caught by shooting. The setting spaniels were used to find the game and point it, and the springing spaniel flushed the game from the cover so that it could be shot.

In the *Sportsman's Cabinet*, written by Nicolas Cox and published in 1803 we find this description of the spaniel: The true-bred, English bred Springer

NEATH VALLEY
In the 18th and 19th centuries, Welsh Spaniels were confined mainly to the Neath Valley in South Wales, where they were bred purely for work.

Spaniel differs but little in figure from the setter, except in size varying only a small degree, if any, from a red, yellow or liver colour and white, which seems to be the invariable external standard of this breed. They are nearly two-fifths less in height and strength than the Setter, delicately formed, ears long, soft and pliable, coat waving and silky, eyes and nose red or black, the tail bushy and pendulous, always in motion when actively employed. Other indirect evidence of the existence of red and white dogs can be found in the 18th century work *A Treatise on Field Diversions* by the Reverend B Symonds of Kelsale, Suffolk. He mentions two coat colours, black tanned and orange or lemon and white and two types, short and long waved coats.

On a painting of James Howe (1780–1836), now in the possession of The Kennel Club, we see the famous Scots falconer James

ON A STAMP
The Welsh Springer Spaniel is featured on stamps in many countries, but the best one is probably the one issued by the General Post Office in Great Britain. It is a 10 1/2 pence stamp, featuring *Tarfgi Cymreig* by the artist Peter Barrett.

Anderson surrounded by six dogs, among whom are small, red and white Spaniels.

In the 18th century, the term springing spaniel was gaining ground as a description, not of a particular variety but of the group of gundogs that sprung their game. All land spaniels came under this heading and the varieties we now know as Clumber, Welsh and English Springer, Field, Cocker and Sussex Spaniel were all springing spaniels.

Although it appears that the red and white spaniel was well distributed throughout Britain at one time, during the 18th and 19th centuries they were confined mainly to the Neath Valley in

Sh Ch Progress of Pencelli, bred and owned by Harold Newman in the mid-1970s.

South Wales.

Evidence thereof is found in the book *Dogs in Britain* by Clifford Hubbard, renowned authority on dogs and he wrote, 'The spaniels of Wales were almost all red and white, and it is certain that the Welsh Springer Spaniel is descended from a type which was common to Wales and seldom found elsewhere till comparatively recent years.'

Mr A T Williams, who was to play such an important part in the founding of the breed, told of his

> **A 'STARTER'**
> Another name for the Welsh Springer is 'starter' which is derived from 'to start,' meaning to spring the game. Its Welsh equivalent, 'tarfgi,' is more commonly used in Wales than the term 'Springer'.

family using Welsh Spaniels for sporting purposes. They were very uniform in type but varying in colour. The flesh-coloured nose was considered to be more correct than the black, whereas today the standard requires nostrils to be brown or dark and the coat rich red and white only. Still, flesh-coloured noses and lighter shades of red are sometimes seen.

In the many years that Welsh Spaniels were bred in the Neath Valley of Wales, they were bred purely for work, although they

Sh Ch Dalati Del, bred and owned by Mr and Mrs N Hunton-Morgans, winning at Crufts in 1973.

Maud Earl's lovely painting from 1906 depicting Mrs H D Greene's Ch Longmynd Calon Fach and Ch Longmynd Megan.

Sh Ch Contessa of Tregwillym, circa 1976.

crossbreeding was done regularly in the first decade of the century.

The real Welsh Springer history probably begins with Corrin, who was born in 1893 and who competed successfully in the show ring with all other kinds of sporting spaniels. He was bred by Colonel Blandy-Jenkins of Lhanharan and was owned by Mr A T Williams ('Gerwn'). Although Corrin himself was registered as a Welsh Cocker, born of two red and white parents, his offspring was variously registered. Bred to Mena of Gerwn, he produced Rover of Gerwn, probably Mr Williams's best Welsh Springer and, after the breed had been recognised as a separate variety, the first Welsh Springer Spaniel champion. Rover, bred to Belle of Gerwn, produced Duke of Gerwn, who was black and white, and Roverson of Gerwn, who was liver and white. Both of them can be found in the pedigrees of

were also seen at shows. There were classes for Welsh Spaniels and Land Spaniels of any variety, but there was much variation.

The spaniel situation was a mixed bag, with offspring of English Springers being registered as Field Spaniel or Welsh Spaniel according to their size and/or colour and Cockers and Field Spaniels being born in the same litter, registered according to their weight.

Crossbreeding had always occurred in working circles, but links between the newly separated breeds of spaniel were open and

A WORK OF ART

In 1999, the Crufts catalogue, schedules and posters, all carried a reproduction of a painting of two Welsh Springers Spaniels by Maud Earl (1864-1943), namely Ch Longmynd Myfanwy and Ch Longmynd Megan. Both were born in 1904, bred and owned by Mrs H D Greene and were big winners in their day. The original painting is in the possession of The Kennel Club and on display in its London office.

American and Canadian field trial English Springers.

Mr A J Dyke started his strain of Welsh with a bitch Floss of Mont, registered as a Welsh Springer but she had a red and white Cocker as a sire and a liver and white English Springer as a dam.

In 1902, it was Mr Williams who, together with a group of Welsh gentlemen that included Colonel Blandy-Jenkins, of 'Lhanharan' and breeder of Corrin, offered the evidence to The Kennel Club that the Welsh Springer Spaniel was a separate breed, different from the English Springer Spaniel. Mr Williams, who could trace his family's kennel back to the end of the 18th century, and the other gentlemen could affirm that this breed of dog had been kept for many years in their families' kennels. Mr Williams's plea was successful and the Welsh Springer Spaniel was recognised as a separate variety by The Kennel Club in 1902.

Although the Lhanharan kennel disappeared, its name still lives in the lozenge shaped red spot, found so often on top of the head between the red ears, traditionally called the Lhanharan spot.

Soon after recognition, the Welsh Spaniel Club was founded. The first secretary was Mrs H D Greene of Longmynd. Her prefix

still lives on in the most famous breed picture by Maud Earl in 1906, which depicts two of her champions, Ch Longmynd Calon Fach and Ch Longmynd Megan.

Although the breed did fairly well, being popular as a working dog, breed activities came to a halt in 1914 when the First World War broke out. After the war it was Colonel Downes-Powell who revived the activities and formed a new club, the Welsh Springer

Sh Ch Dalati Sarian winning at the 1987 Championship Show.

Sh Ch Plattburn Pinetree, bred and owned by Mr J K Burgess, pictured here in 1977.

Outstanding dogs of this period were F Morris's Ch Barglam Bang, Colonel Downes-Powell's Ch Marksman o'Matherne and Ch Musketeer o'Matherne, and Mr A J Dyke's Ch Marglam Maquis. It must be remembered that in order to become a champion in those days a dog had to win on the bench and in the field as well.

Just before the Second World War, three new breeders started,

Spaniel Club.

The club set out to safeguard the dual-purpose ideal as much as possible and emphasis was placed on working qualities. The number of Welsh Springers registered yearly in the years between the two World Wars was around 100 but there might well have been many more, living as pets or working dogs, that were not registered. At the shows between 10 and 20 Welsh were entered, increasing to 30 to 40 just before the Second World War. The centre of activity was still based in Wales.

Mr Harold Newman (Pencelli) and Mr Cliff Payne (Tregwillym) in the early 1970s.

notably Harold Newman (Pencelli), Cliff Payne (Tregwillym) and Hal Leopard (Rushbrooke), who would have, as history proves, a tremendous influence on the breed.

Mr Leopard's bitch, Goitre Lass, had nine litters and her name can be seen in quite a few pedigrees. According to Mr Leopard, who thought Goitre Lass came from a Cocker or English Springer mating, she was the origin of the dark-nosed strain of Welsh Springer. For a long time, pink noses and hazel eyes as well

Sh Ch Hillpark Mr Polly, bred and owned by Mr and Mrs J S Walton, pictured at Crufts in 1976.

as dark noses and dark eyes were seen, and it is believed that Goitre Lass progeny started this fashion for dark noses, which is the preferred colour nowadays.

The Second World War was

Sh Ch Dalati Rhian.

Mr Howard Newman (Pencelli) was largely responsible for the continuation of the breed following the Second World War. When he passed away in 1980, he had been in the breed for over 50 years.

kennels of Cliff Payne started to dominate the ring. Token, Top Score of Tregwillym, Statesman of Tregwillym and T Trigger became champions. Token of Tregwillym was top dog in 1956 and again in 1957 when it tied with Top Score of Tregwillym.

not as damaging to the breed as The Great War, as there were more dogs with the majority of them being in South Wales, which was less threatened by the war than London and the Midlands.

Colonel Downes-Powell ('the Colonel') more or less kept the club going. It turned out to be an extremely wise move when he asked Harold Newman officially to continue the breed, a nomination of which Harold was very proud. Harold, who already had had some success in the 1930s with Barmaid and Sh Ch Dere Mhlaen, concentrated purely on the show ring, but breeders such as Mrs Marjorie Mayall and A J Dyke remained dual-purpose enthusiasts and safeguarded the working abilities of the breed.

In the 1950s the Tregwillym

Sh Ch Wainfelin Barly Mo, winner of 41 CCs.

Sh Ch Highclare Rorkes Drift (left) and Sh Dalville Dancing Water, handled by breeder Ruth Dalrymple.

By that time The Kennel Club had decided to introduce the title of Show Champion for a dog that had won three Challenge Certificates (CCs); Champion for the dog that had won three CCs and had also qualified in the field; and Dual Champion for a dog that has obtained the title of Show Champion and Field Trial Champion as well.

Sh Ch Russethill Royal Salute over Nyliram winning from the veteran class in 1998.

Mr and Mrs Morgans sold their Brancourt kennel to Mr T Hubert Arthur, who already was a noted Cocker breeder and his Sh Ch Brancourt Belinda was top bitch in 1958, 1959 and 1960. One of the first Welsh Springers to win group honours was Ann West's Deri Darrell of Linkhill (by Statesman) who was Reserve in the Gundog Group at Crufts three times and won a Best in Show in 1964.

Golden Tint of Tregwillym (by Sportsman of Tregwillym) started winning his tickets in 1965 and ended up as a record breaker with 33 CCs.

In 1967 the Plattburn kennels started to attract attention. The breeder, Ken Burgess made up

Paramount and Penny, and Progressor became top dog in 1971. Burgess exported many quality dogs to countries such as the Netherlands, Australia and Scandinavia where they formed, together with Dalati exports, the basis for the 'modern type' of the breed.

The 1960s and '70s were good years for the breed. Clever breeders managed to keep the type and quality intact, but although the club continued to encourage work and show, the emphasis among the members increasingly turned to the shows. The field trial enthusiasts eventually decided to move away to a separate field trial club, established by Mr Leopard.

Throughout this period the breed started to grow in numbers. The breed popularity could be

seen at the shows as there were more CCs on offer and the class sizes and total show entry increased, making competition quite keen. The '70s and '80s were truly golden years for the Welsh Springer Spaniel with an abundance of quality and type and names that cannot be forgotten. Harold Newman, Cliff Payne, Noel and Dodo Hunton-Morgans ('Dalati'), Maggie Mullins

The author, judging UK breed record holder Sh Ch Russethill Royal Salute Over Nyliram.

Sh Ch Ferndel Cecilia (left) and Sh Ch Hillpark Music of the Night in 1999.

Sh Ch Dalati
Sioni, 1983,
top producer
in the breed.

('Athelwood') and Gordon
Pattinson ('Tidemarsh') all came
into the ring with unforgettable
dogs. Plattburn Perchance,
Progress, Pinetree and Peewit
(who later went to the Nether-
lands), Dalati Del, top bitch in
1972 and 1973 (in a tie with
Tregwillym Golden Gem),
Contessa of Tregwillym, who won
Best in Show at the Welsh Kennel
Club show in 1975.

It was definitely a loss for the
Welsh Springer fraternity when in
1980, at the age of only 69, after
51 years of activity as a breeder
and exhibitor, Harold Newman
passed away.

H Cliff Payne's influence on
the breed has been widespread.
He was a defender of the working
qualities of the breed, a shooting

enthusiast and a leader and
adviser for other breeders. Over
the years he won over 150 CCs
with his dogs, 30 of them won by
Sh Ch Contessa of Tregwillym
alone. Dogs of his breeding
became the foundation stock for
kennels such as Athelwood,
Brent, Bramblebank, Hillpark,
Krackton, Tidemarsh and
Wainfelin. His exports such as Sh
Ch Trigger of Tregwillym to USA,
Sh Ch Nobleman to Finland and
Sh Ch Golden Gem to New
Zealand not only were world
famous but also became the
foundation stock for the breed in
these countries.

A special mention must be
made of the Dalati Welsh
Springers of Noel and Dodo
Hunton-Morgans. They started in
the 1960s and over the years
produced many champions of
whom Sh Ch Dalati Del, top bitch
in 1972 and 1973 (in a tie with Sh
Ch Tregwillym Golden Gem), Sh
Ch Dalati Sioni and Sh Ch Dalati
Sarian deserve special mention.
Sioni himself won 18 CCs but he
is the top producer in the breed
with 23 Sh Ch offspring. He died,
at the age of 14, in 1996. Sarian,
by Sh Ch Tregwillym Royal Mint,
was a group winner at Crufts and
won a total of 37 CCs.

Sh Ch Wainfelin Barley Mo,
also by Tregwillym Royal Mint,
bred and owned by Mansel and
Averil Young, was for a long time
breed record holder with 41 CCs

until Sh Ch Russethill Royal Salute over Nyliram, by Sh Ch Dalati Sioni, bred by Doreen Gately and owned by Tom Graham, came along. 'Harvey' was top Welsh Springer in 1992, 1993 and 1994. With a total of 58 CCs, he is still the breed record holder.

Sh Ch Northoaks Sea Mist of Menstionia, bred by Christopher Anderson and owned by Christine Knowles, was top bitch in 1991, 1992 and 1993 and top Welsh in 1995.

Nowadays there are many more successful kennels such as Cwrt Afon (Len and Kate Morgan), Northey (Christine Mc Donald) Taimere (Graham and Lesley Tain), Weslave (John and Joy Hartley), Parkmist (Trudy and Bill Short), Kazval (Frank Whyte) Julita (Julie Revill), Highclare (Gill Tully) and Ferndel (John Thirwell). His first champion was Dalati Gwent but he bred an impressive number of champions of whom Ferndell Stroller became famous as a stud dog and Ferndel Cecilia was probably the one who gained her title quickest. She needed just three shows to win 3 CCs and ended up as top Welsh Springer in 1999. In 1996 and 1998 he successfully showed Sh Ch Dalville Dancing Water (by Ferndel Dancing Brave), a bitch he co-owned with her breeder, Ruth Dalrymple. She was Best in Show at the Ladies Kennel Club show in 1997.

Ferndel Cecilia was top bitch and top Welsh in 1999; Hillpark Music of the Night, bred by Anne Walton, was top dog in 1999.

The breed has grown in popularity and, thanks to quality exports, also thrives in many countries, notably Scandinavia, Netherlands, France, USA, Australia and New Zealand.

With his temperament and character, his pearly white and red coat, his handy size and general appearance, it is no wonder that so many people in so many countries consider the Welsh Springer Spaniel as one of the most attractive dogs in the world.

THE WELSH SPRINGER SPANIEL AROUND THE WORLD

The Welsh Springer Spaniel has an international network of breed devotees, who often know each other personally or who keep in

Sh Ch Dalati Sarian winning the Gundog Group and Reserve Best in Show at Crufts in 1990.

Sh Ch Tregwillym Golden Gem with breeder Mr Cliff Payne in 1975. Golden Gem went to Australia in 1978 and became, along with her grandson, the foundation of Nantyderi kennels.

touch through the Internet. You will find many international websites and sometimes even a virtual breed show where the dogs are being judged in classes like a real dog show.

AUSTRALIA AND NEW ZEALAND

We know that some Welsh Springers were exported to Australia before the Second World War, but no records could be found and it is likely that these dogs were not used for breeding purposes. The real history started in 1973 when Mr and Mrs S Jeffery ('Talgarth') imported Plattburn Paceman and Plattburn Pi, bred by Ken Burgess in Great Britain. This successful pair formed the start of the breed in Australia.

Sue and Jim Simmonds ('Pennlyon') purchased Talgarth Temptation, who had two litters from which seven puppies later became champions. Talgarth Tasha, litter sister to Temptation also became a champion and she produced three Australian champions. All these litters were sired by Pencelli Prospect, who not only sired nine litters in which he produced 27 Australian Champions and a New Zealand champion but who also was very successful in the ring, winning 16 groups, a Reserve Best in Show and a Best in Show.

Talgarth Cassandra, owned by Bobbie Hitchcock, was mated to Pencelli Prospect to produce the first Rhywderin litter, and Tess Hay's Brynderyn kennels are founded on Rhywderin and Pennlyon stock.

In 1978 Scott and Eira Taylor imported Sh Ch Trygwillym Golden Gem and her grandson Tregwillym Taliesin. These two were the start of the Nantyderi kennels and these imports can be found in many pedigrees.

In New Zealand Mr and Mrs P Lawless based their Bryndoain kennels in New Zealand on Northey blood.

In 1982 a breed club was formed. A number of Open Shows are held annually and since 1989 two Championship Shows have been held every year.

CANADA

Registered in 1949, the first Welsh Springer Spaniels in Canada were Countess Hobo of Dale and Prince Bohunk, but nothing was heard from them or their owner, Mr Kirkpatrick of Ontario.

In 1969 Eve Carter of Ontario imported Rona of Pencelli who, in whelp to Nobleman of Tregwillym, became the foundation bitch of her Ghost Inn kennel.

Peggy Saltman ('Coedmawr') imported Ceinwen of Tregwillym in 1962, the third Welsh to be registered with the Canadian Kennel Club and the first to gain his title. She bought Ghost Inn Peredur but all her attempts to breed Ceinwen to Peredur failing, she imported Tregwillym Merionwen. The resulting three litters from that bitch and Peredur were the beginning of her Coedmawr kennel which proved to be the foundation of several kennels in Western Canada and of two thirds of all the Canadian Welsh Springers.

The Roseraie kennel of Andree Plante started in 1975

Pictured at the 1991 National Speciality of the Welsh Springer Spaniel Club of America (WSSCA) are (from left to right): Mr John Phillips, a judge from the UK; Mrs Carol Krohn with Am Ch Tydaky's Wildfire; Mrs Susan Rhiese, president of the WSSCA and Mrs Ria Hörter, breeder from the Netherlands. Mrs Hörter was the breeder of Valentijn van Snellestein, a very influential import into the USA and a top producer.

with two bitches, imported from Great Britain and a Coedmawr dog. Six litters were born and most of the puppies were shown. However, in 1977, Andree Plante decided to stop breeding and showing after six of her dogs perished in a fire which destroyed her home.

Bankdam's Taffy Bark was the first champion for Gordon Wilkinson, later followed by Coedmawr Megan of Bankdam and Pencelli Pandour. Taffy, bred to Megan, produced the top Welsh

> **RECOGNITION**
> The Welsh Springer Spaniel was recognised by The Kennel Club in 1902 and by the American Kennel Club as early as 1906.

ever bred in Canada, Can & Am Ch Bankdam's Bobby Dazzler, whose influence in the breed is still felt. The top Welsh in Canada in 1993, 1994 and 1995 and the top Welsh in the U.S. in 1994 and 1995, the best bitch at the WSSCA National Speciality in 1995 and America's top obedience Welsh two years running were all great-grandchildren of Bobby Dazzler.

UNITED STATES

In the United States the breed was formally recognised by the American Kennel Club (AKC) in 1906 although red and white spaniels have been seen in earlier illustrations or paintings. The Mississippi Valley KC show (April 1911) recorded an entry of four Welsh Springer Spaniels, all owned by Mr A A Busch.

The first Welsh Springer Spaniel to be registered was Faircroft Bob (great-grandson of Ch Longmynd Calon Fach) owned and bred by Harry B Hawes in 1914 as was his sire Faircroft Snip and four littermates. His dam, Faircroft Sue was registered in 1915. Until 1929 only a handful were registered and between 1929

Am Ch Royailes Cool Ham Luke, pictured following his Best in Show at a 1996 show in the USA.

> **THE FIRST MEMBER**
> Mr I J Smith from the USA was the first overseas member of the Welsh Springer Spaniel Club of Great Britain in 1950.

Pictured at the 1994 WSSCA Speciality, from left to right: Mrs Anne Walton, a judge from the UK; Mrs Marta Stoneman with Ch Statesman Lhanharans Abbey and Mrs Susan Rhiese, WSSCA president and breeder of Abbey.

SHOW TIME

In the United States, Welsh Springers were being shown ten years before there were classes available for English Springers.

and 1949 none at all.

This doesn't mean there were no Welsh Springer Spaniels at all, because there were. They were owned by sportsmen as hunting companions and were either unregistered or registered in the American Field Stud Book, a working gundog registry not affiliated with the AKC. Until the 50s

they were acquired, bred and kept purely as working dogs.

One of these early supporters of the breed was Hobart Ames of Connecticut who imported his shooting dogs from the kennels of A T Williams. One of the last of the Lhanharran strain, Marged O'Matherne, was imported in the 1920s by a sportsman in the Midwest.

Probably the most famous introduction of the breed to America came in 1950 when Dorothy Ellis and four of her adult Downland Welsh and a puppy flew from England to New York to exhibit at Westminster, Hartford and Boston. At each show one of her dogs was Best of Breed and they received much attention and publicity. She went home without the dogs, having sold them to breed fanciers; the first American Champion, Ch Holiday of Happy Hunting, was a son of two of these imports.

In the early '60s, Bert and Edna Randolph of Randhaven

Ch. Rysan's First Round Kayo, CDX, shown winning Best of Breed at a US show in 1990.

Ch Fracas Little Caesar, winning Best of Breed in the WSSCA Show in 1986.

Ch Bel Canto Remington Gunfire, a typical American champion.

kennels owned or bred eight American champions. They also hired a handler to assist them in showing their rare breed. This

handler was D Lawrence (Laddie) Carswell. Laddie imported Eng Sh Ch Trigger of Tregwillym in 1962. He set out to introduce the breed and to educate the judges and the public on the breed which earned him the nickname 'Mr Welsh Springer Spaniel.' When he died in 1995, the breed lost a great expert and staunch supporter.

The Welsh Springer Spaniel Club was founded in 1961 but it was in the 1970s that the breed started its rise in popularity. Welsh Springers were found across the USA. Imports from

Dutch and German Ch Valentijn van Snellestein, a very influential import and top producer in 1985.

Brent, Pencelli, Hillpark and Tregwillym moulded with American stock to form the foundation for many of today's breeding programs, together with later imports from Scandinavia and the Netherlands. The most influential export has been Dutch and German Ch Valentijn van Snellestein, who was top producer in 1985.

The first club show was held in 1980, where Best in Show was Ch Randail Taffy of Sylabru, whose pedigree could be traced back to the Downland dogs. The second time she won Best of Breed at the club show was from the Veteran Class.

In 1986, when the club celebrated its 25th anniversary, Ch Fracas Little Caesar, bred and owned by Frances and Carl Bloom, and the son of two British imports, Ch Hillpark Brutus and Ch My Fanwy Fair of Hillpark, was Best of Breed. Handled by Laddie Carswell, Fracas Little Caesar became the first Welsh to win an all-breed Best in Show in America, the first and only one to date to win Best in Show at the American Spaniel Club show where all the spaniel varieties compete. Some 37 years after Dorothy Ellis came to Madison Square Garden, Little Caesar was also the first Welsh Springer Spaniel and the only one to win a place in the group at Westminster in the 20th century.

Tydaky's Windfall, winner of the Sweepstakes at the 1997 American speciality show.

Am. Can. Ch Brafci True Colors, two-time speciality winner.

Gallois Thuri, by Sh Ch Ferndel Paper Moon, bred and owned by Finn Nielsen and Merethe Anderson of Denmark.

Danish Ch Booze Boleyn van Berken-stein, bred in the Nether-lands by Monique Huis in't Veld and owned by Lena Sorensen.

Ch Rysan's First Round Kayo, bred and owned by Sandy Rohrbacher, was a multiple Best in Show winner, who was twice Best of Breed at the Welsh Springer Spaniel Club National Speciality as was Ch Bel Canto's Remington Gunfire, bred and owned by Hubler-Ing.

Ch Tydaki's Wildfire, bred and owned by Carol and Maurice Krohn, won the Speciality in 1991 under John Phillips, breed specialist, from Great Britain.

American and Canadian Ch Brafci's True Colors CD also won the National Speciality twice. Furthermore, he won in one and the same year Best of Breed at the American Spaniel Club, at Westminster and at the National Speciality. In 1999 he won again Best of Breed at the American Spaniel Club from the Veteran Class. 'Quincy' is bred and owned by Tonia and Paul Farnell.

Other imports that have done a lot of winning and were of great influence on the breed were Ch Hillpark Caesar and Ch Hillpark Brutus, Ch Pencelli Thomas and Ch Dalati Marc.

At this moment the breed is carefully guided by the breeders on health, quality, temperament and versatility as the interest in the working side is still increasing.

Booze's (right) litter sister Blessed Boleyn van Berken-stein (left) stayed in the Netherlands, where she became a champion.

DENMARK

The Hoje Mon kennel, owned by Ingelise and Ivan Selberg, was the first Welsh Springer kennel in Denmark. Ingelise and Ivan imported Maroon Lotta from Sweden and Dalati Denol and Dalati Dyma Fi from Great Britain in 1974 and 1975.

Brynmore van Snellestein was imported into Denmark from the Netherlands.

Rosa van Snellestein was also imported into Denmark from the Netherlands.

Mette and Lars Kruuse founded the Sweet Chester kennel and Kirsten Hahn and Ove Noraett the Danebod kennel. They imported Triggers Osborne from Sweden and Brynmore and Rosa van Snellestein from the Netherlands, making the breeding foundation in Denmark a combination of Swedish and Dutch bloodlines.

In 1990 Lena Sorensen (Blazewood) imported Booze Boleyn van Berkenstein. Booze became the breed record holder and won a Best in Show at the breed club championship show in the Netherlands. Lena also imported Hillpark Sweet Song.

Birte Bjorn started her Red and White kennel in 1987 with Danebod's Diana Bianca who was very successful in the show ring and in the field. She also imported Nikita Boleyn van Berkenstein.

Merethe Anderson and Finn Nielsen started their Gallois kennel in 1989 and imported Cwrt Afon Harri. Their more recent

The Danish Trigger's Osborne, originally from Sweden.

International,
Finnish and
Norwegian Ch
Delkins Turul
is Marjo
Jaakkola's
extremely
successful
import into
Finland.

import from Sweden, Hammelgardens Original and Best, had great influence on the breed in Denmark.

In order to have a new bloodline, in 1991 French Duke des Terres Froides was imported from France. Since then, Welsh Springers have been imported from various countries and bloodlines vary.

In recent years some Welshies have competed at field trials and some breeders have become more aware of the importance of this dual purpose dog.

FINLAND

Mrs Misse Puolakkainen was the first to introduce the breed in

Finland. She imported two Mustala bitches, two sisters by Plattburn Pimlico, from Sweden in 1967. The first two litters in 1968 were the beginning of the successful 'Skyway' prefix and the foundation of the breed in

The Finnish dog Ch Rwyn King Lear is both a Danish and Finnish champion, and was bred by Mrs Tina Mattila.

champions. One of them, Sprightly Xylophone, was the most successful prize-winning Welsh ever in Finland.

In the 1970s, Tuuliki and Reino Makitalo started the 'Sinsir' kennel with a bitch from Sweden bred on Brent lines.

Leila Kärkäs established the 'Mandeville' kennel and bred the champions Roger Ribbons, Ragtime Rudy, and Roland Rabbit, all by Delkens Turul.

Ch Mandeville Roger Ribbons (left) and Ch Real Braf Cassiopea, both by Ch Delkens Turul, pictured at the Turku Topdog Show, Finland, in 1993.

Finland. In 1969 she imported Ambassador of Tregwillym and Nobleman of Tregwillym and the bitch Golden Charm of Tregwillym, followed in 1975 by Dalati Dyma Fi who turned out to be a very good stud dog. His excellent breed type was passed on to many of his successful offspring.

In 1984 Delkens Turul came to Marjo Jaakkola ('Benton'). He can be considered to be the most important sire in the breed and founder of the breed as it is today in Finland. Not only was he himself a top winner, but he also sired over 30 champions. Indeed, Marjo Jaakkola is one of Finland's top breeders.

Two breeders started with Dalati Dyma Fi offspring: Mrs Tina Mattila 'Rwyn' and Terttu and Hannu Suonto 'Sprightly.' Tina Mattila can be considered to be the most successful breeder of Welsh Springer Spaniels in Finland, having bred over 50 champions, many international champions and top winners.

Mr Hannu Suonto, of the Sprightly kennel, bred several

SWEDEN

The first Welsh Springer Spaniel was Linkhill Five-to-One who was imported in 1963 by Marianne Hermelin 'Mustela'. She was a very successful bitch and her first litter to Gay Boy of Tregwillym gave the breed a very good start.

Anita Norberg 'Himledalen' imported Tidemarsh Ruff, who had a lot of influence on the breed in Sweden.

Metzgard's Fun for the Future, bred by Rita and Bjorn Roger in Norway. She was best bitch at the Swedish Welsh Springer Spaniel Club's show in 1992.

Pencelli Mwyn, imported into Sweden by Birgitta Thoresson.

Mrs Grant Carlson ('Corydon') started in the '60s. She imported four dogs, the most important of whom were Ch Rebecca of Basildon and Benefactor of Brent.

The Swedish Welsh Springer Dalati Curig.

Catarina Hultgren ('Trigger') started in 1971. Trigger Bonny Lass is the only Field Trial Champion in Sweden. She has been very successful over the years in showing, obedience and field trials.

Margareta Edman ('Clumbrolds') started in 1976 on the lines of Corydon. She imported Welsh Guide of Tregwillym, who was the sire of Int SFN Ch Clumbrolds Purpurdöd, the only Welsh to win Best in Show at an all-breed

Championship Show. He was exported to Finland where he had a great influence on the breed.

'Merry One,' the kennel that Bjorn and Yvonne Skeppstedt Schill started in 1985, has been successful in all fields.

Carine Arvidsson started the 'Freckles' kennel in 1986 with a Triggers bitch. Freckles Inspiration became the top field-trial dog in the breed and Freckles Miss Decibell the Best All-Rounder in 1995.

Birgitta Thoresson imported a

few of Harold Newman's dogs when he died. The most influential and successful was Pencelli Mwyn who put a mark on the breed in the '80s. He was a top winner and was twice Best in Show at the club show.

Karin Brostam and Anita Högström of the Don's kennels started in 1989 with Weslave Winter Breeze and Ch Metzgard's Moonlight Valley, who became the top winning Welsh ever. He was twice Best in Show at the club show, and had several Best in Show wins at championship

Ch Don's Thunderstorm was the top Welsh Springer in Sweden in 1993.

She imported Dalati Curig and several very successful Rwyn Welsh Springers from Finland.

'Hillcrofts' was founded in 1990 by Agneta and Bert Mansson. They started with Clumbrolds Trollslanda and have been doing very well. Laila Gistedt started her Designer's kennels in the mid-nineties.

NORWAY

The first Welsh Springer Spaniel came to Norway in 1970 but it was not until the eighties that serious breeding began by Rita and Bjørn Gran with the Metzgard kennel. They imported Hasselholm's Isabella from Sweden and Delkens Troydon from England and from this combination came their most famous dog Ch

shows, one of them being the Centenary Show of the Swedish Kennel Club in 1989, the biggest show ever in Sweden. Don's Thunderstorm was a group winner and Top Welsh in 1993.

Gudrun Jonsson's 'Hammel-gardens' kennel started in 1990.

Ch Hammel-gården's Made in Sweden is a European Champion and was Best of Breed at the 1997 European Championship Show in Copenhagen.

Ch Inu-Goya Ferrymaster, multi-group and Best in Show winner in Norway.

Norwegian Ch Metzgard's Moonlight Valley, bred by Rita and Bjorn Roger in Norway and owned by Annica Högström in Sweden.

Kazval Call Collect who is the most winning Welsh in Norway ever. He was Spaniel of the Year in Norway in 1994, 1995, 1996 and 1997 when he was retired from the show ring. The Inu Goya kennel is no longer active.

Although the number of Welsh Springers in Norway is relatively small there are a number of people who still keep them and breed the occasional

Metzgard's Moonlight Valley. He was exported to Sweden, where he formed the foundation of the Don's kennel, together with the bitch Weslave Winter Breeze. The Metzgard kennel stopped its activities in the early nineties but most of the dogs in Norway have Metzgard dogs in their pedigrees.

Dutch Ch Dalati Drew, winning at the Dutch Championship Show in 1979.

The eighties also saw the start of the Inu Goya kennel of Frank Bjerklund and Terje Johnsen. Although they mainly bred English Springers a fair number of Welshies were bred and shown by them. They imported a.o. Ferndel Harvest Gold and Ferndel Fun but their most influential import was

litter and it looks as if there seems to be an increase in the population.

NETHERLANDS

The first Welsh Springer Spaniel to be registered and shown in the Netherlands was Mist (Longmynd Morgan x Longmynd Myfandy) born in 1908, bred by Mrs H D Greene. Mist literally disappeared in the mist, because after having

Dutch Ch Plattburn Proclaim in 1974.

been shown a couple of times (and winning his classes), no further traces have been found of him. The next entry in the Studbook was a litter out of Beechgrove Trust by Colwyn Colonist, registered as English Springers. One of the puppies, Good Luck's Boy, was registered and shown as a red and white Welsh Springer Spaniel.

After that we find no more mention of Welsh Springer Spaniels till 1950, when Red Rascal of Downland, bred by Mrs D H Ellis, came to the Netherlands and Mrs S E van Boetzelaer imported Rushbrooke Rhoda, bred by Mr H J H. Leopard. Rhoda's first litter by Red Rascal was registered under the Riverland prefix. In the following years the number of Welsh Springers slowly but gradually increased from 1

Dutch Ch Plattburn Pinecob, bred by Mr J K Burgess and owned by Mr J van Elteren in the early 1970s.

litter in 1959 to 29 litters in 1999.

Influential imports in those early days were Rushbrooke Ringer, Dalati Delwen and Jonathan of Brent. In the early '70s, Plattburn Pinecone was imported, in whelp by Plattburn Perchance. One of the pups, Isselsteyn's Cita, became a champion and produced many more champions mated to Dalati Aled and later to Dalati Drew. Another dog that had great influence on the breed was Reliance of Krackton, who did not gain a title himself but sired four champions. One of the British kennels that probably contributed most significantly in the foundation of the breed in the Netherlands was the Plattburn kennel of Ken Burgess. Later quality imports from Pencelli and Dalati helped to

Sh Ch and Dutch Ch Bramblebank Calamity Jane, bred by Mrs V Roach and later owned by Mrs Ria Hörter, here seen winning at Crufts in 1978.

The only Welsh Springer to win a best in show in the Netherlands: multi-champion Northoaks Sea Sun Flower, owned by Marie Madeleine van Grinsven.

Aled x Isselsteyn's Cita) mated to Lennart of Speldermark produced the first Snellestein champion. The second champion was Valentijn of Snellestein (Reliance of Krackton x Bramblebank Calamity Jane). He went to the United States in the mid '80s, where he had a successful showcareer and proved to be a valuable stud dog. He came back after a couple of years to resume his successful show career as a veteran. Ria stopped her breeding in 1984 but came back a few years later and with her new prefix 'of Rowan's Residence' regained her position as one of the Dutch top breeders. Her greatest success came with the import Nyliram Mr Dark Horse (by breed record holder Russethill Royal Salute over Nyliram) who was top Welsh Springer in the Netherlands for three years. Wesley of Rowan's Residence (by Mapleby Post

build a strong line.

One of the most important kennels was undoubtedly Ria Lissenberg-Hörter's (now Hörter) 'Van Snellestein'. Her success started with the import of Sh Ch Bramblebank Calamity Jane in 1978. She represented a different type of Welsh Springer and offered the much needed new bloodline. Isselsteyn's Iris (Dalati

Mr Ken Burgess (second from the left) judging at the Welsh Springer Spaniel Club Show in the Netherlands.

Dutch Ch Blessed Boleyn van Berkenstein, bred by Monique Huis In't Veld and owned by Mrs Ria Hörter.

Master) was top Welsh and reserve top gundog in 1998.

Monique Huis In't Veld, 'van Berkenstein', had a very good start with Wainfelin Miss Money Penny. Mated to Dalati Sinsir she produced her first champion and, mated to a son of Sinsir, she produced another champion. Over the years this kennel has produced a number of top winning Welsh Springers and several champions. Nicolaas van Snellestein was the sire of the first 'Schokkerwaard' champion of breeders Henk Stalknecht and Nienke de Vries. Julia Huckley van 't Schokkerwaard herself produced two champions.

A more recent kennel is 'Inma.' Owner Ine van den Beuken bred her first litter in 1987. She is one of the most successful breeders in the Netherlands, having bred quite a number of champions. Her top-winning bitch to date is Inma's Nimble Nidian, who won several groups and Reserve Bests in Show and ended up as top Welsh Springer and top Gundog in 1999.

Another successful breeder is

Dutch and Luxembourg Ch Nicolaas van Snellestein in the mid-1980s.

Top Welsh
Springer and
Top Gundog in
the Nether-
lands in 1999
was Dutch Ch
Inma's Nimble
Nidian, bred
and owned by
Ine van de
Beuken.

The top Welsh Springer in the Netherlands in 1998 was
Dutch Ch Wesley of Rowan's Residence, bred and
owned by Mrs Ria Hörter.

Marie Madeleine van Grinsven,
'Of the Yasmin Garden,' who bred
her first litter in 1988. She has
bred several champions at the
time of writing, but her greatest
success came with the import
Northoak's Sea Sun Flower, who
won many titles and was the first
Welsh Springer to win a Best in
Show at an all-breed Championship Show in the Netherlands.

Fortunately, there is a growing
interest in the working side and
two Welsh Springers have
succeeded in winning the coveted
title of International Champion by
winning at shows and at a field
trial.

FRANCE

The first breeder of Welsh
Springer Spaniels in France was
Dr Drouillard, a Cocker breeder
who imported Peridot of Tarbay
in whelp to Sh Ch Mikado of
Broomleaf in 1958. The bitch
Hilda du Valcain went to L R
Veignat who bred her to Myrddin

From France, a group of Welshies 'Des Fretillants,' bred
and owned by Mr L R Veignat in 1980.

The top Dutch
Welsh Springer
for three consec-
utive years was
Dutch Ch
Nyliram Mr Dark
Horse, bred by
Mr T Graham in
Great Britain
and owned by
Mrs Ria Hörter.

Niclas van Snellestein (brother of Nicolaas) went to the United States where he became an American champion.

THIRD
IN GROUP

SPORTING

SALINAS VALLEY

KENNEL CLUB
APRIL 1985

Dewi-Brigitte and Dagobert des Terres Froides.

Dewr. A bitch from that combination, Merry des Fretillants, was bred to Deri Day of Linkhill and produced Pat and Porros des Frétillants and Quetzal des Frétillants in a repeat mating. They were all very successful in the show and in the field.

Sharlotte des Frétillants went to Brigitte Bolzea ('des Terres Froides'). Her offspring was very successful in the ring and did a lot to help the breed along. She was mated to Ch Idris Cymro van Snellestein twice which resulted in 6 champions who, in turn,

French and International Ch Chadock des Terres Froides, bred and owned by Mrs B Bolzea.

produced champions.

Although French breeding is of top quality, there are not many Welsh Springers in France. A French Show Champion must have gained a qualification in a field trial besides its three CACs, and therefore working ability is highly rated and the breeders are very careful to preserve the dual purpose of the breed.

GERMANY

The Welsh Springer has never been a popular breed in Germany and it is only in recent years that interest in the breed has developed. In the 60s and 70s it was mainly Harry Hinckeldeyn ('Hinckeldeyn's') and Renate Wulff ('von der Grauen Stadt') who kept the breed going. Jürgen and Lucy Wallat started their 'von der Ruraue' kennels in the early '90s and they successfully try to combine show and work in their breeding programme. Nowadays we see Welsh Springers more often at shows, although not in any great numbers, and there are some imports, mainly from Denmark.

CZECH REPUBLIC

Welsh Springer history in the Czech Republic started in 1963 when Mr Liml imported Hinckeldeyn's Aar (out of Rushbrooke Ringlet) and received Bright Poppet of Hearts, bred in Great Britain from Mr

German, Luxembourg and International Ch Gaston von der Ruraue (left) and German, Luxembourg, Polish and International Ch Jasmin von der Ruraue, bred and owned by Lucy and Jurgen Wallat in Germany.

Hinckeldeyn. This pair had three litters.

Later Hinckeldeyn's Elk (from Germany) and Ugo des Frétillants (from France) came to the country. In the following years more dogs were imported from France, Holland and Sweden.

Since the right to be a breeder was reserved to members of the Union of Czech Hunters, the number of litters was restricted and almost entirely confined to hunters.

Nowadays, travelling is easier and dogs from other countries are used more frequently. By making a test for hunting suitability obligatory for dogs that are being used for breeding, the breeders have succeeded in preserving the working abilities of the breed and Czech puppies, especially from the Jifex kennels, find their way to working and showing enthusiasts in other countries.

Characteristics of the
WELSH SPRINGER SPANIEL

PHYSICAL CHARACTERISTICS
The Welsh Springer Spaniel is a medium-sized, symmetrical, compact dog, and his build is meant for hard work. He is a proper working dog and, as such, has a lot of energy and endurance. His temperament is merry and active, interested in everything that happens, although he is always gentle and never aggressive. It goes without saying that a dog with such a temperament can never be happy in the confines of a small flat with an owner who is at work all day.

Such a dog needs the liveliness of a family and lots of exercise.

The Welsh Springer has a couple of very distinct characteristics. First of all, his colour: rich red and white only, a beautiful combination of a deep and warm colour red and the purest white possible. That means that any shade of orange, brown or yellow is wrong. The pattern of the markings and the quantity of red markings is totally unimportant and just a matter of taste, although for a show dog 'unfortunate' markings

Welshies love to be around their owners and are always ready for a cuddle!

may be a slight handicap. Some people prefer open markings, but saddle-marked dogs are quite often seen and are just as attractive. Another characteristic is his outline: square, compact and slightly arched over the loin. There is little essential difference between the bodies in many varieties of spaniel, apart from this slight arch over the loin. This is a result of the propulsion from the rear, a muscular development and should not be confused with a roached back or a rise towards the rear. Any arch in a different place means that the dog has either a dip behind the shoulder or an uphill rise in the rear. This is a very important characteristic which—together with his lovely colour—distinguishes the Welsh Springer from the other spaniels.

Another distinctive feature is his head, which is very balanced, beautifully chiselled and with eyes that may vary from hazel to dark but must always have that gentle spaniel expression. The ear should be vineleaf shaped. The ear size may vary but for practical reasons a comparatively small ear is preferred.

Fortunately, there is not yet a divergence in type between the working Welsh and the show Welsh. The difference is not as great as that in English Springers or Cockers, for example, and breeders are trying very hard to

combine type and working instincts. Many trainers have reached dual purpose success, but it is a dilemma to try and breed for conservation of working instincts, type and soundness.

Why the breed is fortunate enough not to have a separation of working and show type is not quite clear. It could be because the breed is numerically small and not very fashionable and because there is a good understanding between working and showing fraternity. Also, there is a great deal of determination on the part of many Welsh Springer owners to aim for the dual purpose ideal, in Great Britain as well as on the Continent.

A distinct physical trait of the Welsh Springer is his colour. He must be deep red and pure white; no other colours or shadings are acceptable.

WELSH SPRINGER PERSONALITY
The Welsh Springer Spaniel is a gundog although he is less used for work nowadays. That doesn't

A gundog by nature, the Welsh Springer loves and needs activity. A run (supervised, of course) through a field or in the woods will keep him physically fit and mentally stimulated.

mean, however, that he has lost his working abilities. In many countries people are still training and working their Welshes, and although they have to compete against their talented English Springer cousins, often from working lines, they do manage to hold their own.

Gundogs in general are docile, trainable and ready to serve, loyal and faithful, and they love to be with their humans. They are absolutely devoted to their family. That means that a Welsh should live in the family and be around family members as much as possible. He can be left on his own for a couple of hours, if need be, but only when he has become accustomed to an empty house.

Being a gundog means that a Welsh Springer needs exercise and the excitement of running in a field or the woods and smelling all sorts of highly exciting smells. This will keep him healthy, not only physically, but mentally as well. A gentle stroll in the park is definitely not enough for a dog

Young puppies and young children go together naturally...just be sure that they both know how to behave properly with each other.

with so much stamina and such a strong scenting ability. A Welsh Springer is an alert and intelligent dog with an enquiring mind which means that he can be quite lively and high-spirited. Not only does he require plenty of exercise but also training and education. If his liveliness is not channelled you may end up with a mischievous and destructive dog which you may find very difficult or even impossible to cure. A dog that has plenty of exercise of body and mind will be a happy, relaxed dog in the house who, after his exercise, will love to be curled up near you (preferably on the couch, of course!).

A well-trained Welsh makes a very good pet. He loves company and is very good with children and other dogs. He may be a bit reserved with strangers but he will never show aggressiveness towards them. His happy temperament with the ever-wagging tail makes him fun to be with. However, it should never be forgotten that a Welsh is a spaniel; therefore, obedience may not be one of his stronger points. A gentle but firm hand is an absolute necessity.

You may find there are two types of Welsh: the quiet, friendly and sometimes rather reserved or withdrawn dog (ideal for the

the showring as you can well imagine! It goes without saying that dogs of such different temperaments need different training methods.

Welsh Springers do love to play and they have a sense of humour. He may look gloomy or downright sad with his Spaniel face but he never really is and he delights in fun and play. He loves to play tug of war and hide-and-seek and you can easily teach him basic obedience like sit and stay without him even noticing it! Also retrieving can be taught as fun and games because he loves to carry things in his mouth. Don't punish him for going off with your shoe, but take it gently from him and thank him profusely for giving it back to you. You'll find that after a while he will bring everything he finds back to you and be very proud of it as well. It may be a bit of a nuisance, having

The best of friends...a handsome young Welshie with his handsome young master.

show ring but less ideal for work and obedience training) or the outgoing, exuberant, very active and noisy dog, always friendly and non-aggressive—a disaster in

The Welsh Springer is known worldwide, as many dogs made their way overseas to other countries.

to put back everything where it belongs, but it will teach your dog to retrieve without him realising it. It will also teach you to ensure that there is nothing precious or fragile for him to carry off!

Energy, liveliness, sensitivity, a sense of humour: these are all very positive traits which can turn negative if not used in the right way. Loyalty and protectiveness can turn into sharpness, especially towards other dogs; caution towards strangers can turn into shyness or the capacity to be easily frightened; liveliness can turn into excitability and near-hysteria or a very noisy animal.

Everything really depends on you. Your behaviour and the training you give your dog will determine the kind of dog you are going to have in the future.

Owners do tend to forget this. They come home with this adorable and sweet puppy, with its cute little face. However, this very sweet puppy sets out to discover how far he can go and what is allowed and what not. Moreover, if you allow him to get away with everything in the beginning, you will have a very hard time trying to correct this behaviour. So be wise and keep a tight rein right from the start. Mind you, a tight rein doesn't mean punishment, it just means discipline i.e. being firm and consistent. Teach the puppy to run free without going off, to

come back when called and to walk on a lead without pulling.

A Welsh Springer may bark to warn you that there is something wrong (in his eyes) but don't expect him to be a guard dog. He will let you know with a lot of noise that there is a burglar in the house, but having done that, he will happily show the burglar where you keep the silver.

Bearing in mind the two different kinds of temperament, you have to decide, before you set out to buy a puppy, which type in general you would prefer and what activities you are planning to enjoy with your Welsh.

The difference between a dog

Julita Rainspeckle demonstrates what a Welshie does best.

and bitch is very obvious. A dog is bigger, heavier in bone and in head, whereas a bitch is more refined and elegant. The difference in temperament is not so obvious. Whereas dogs have the reputation of being more difficult, you may find that your dog is a softy and prefers to sleep on your lap. The bitch might be more intolerant and not so even-tempered as the dog. Therefore, the only decisive factor in choosing a dog or a bitch is your personal preference.

When buying a Welsh you should realise that he drops his lovely white and red coat twice a year (some dogs do this the whole year round) and the white hairs,

in particular, are hard to overlook on your dark blue suit.

His nails have to be trimmed and his ears have to be checked on a regular basis. The Welsh Springer Spaniel ears are smaller and finer than those of the other spaniel varieties and they do not tend to cause problems, provided that they are regularly checked and kept trimmed on the inside.

Although few of today's Welsh Springer Spaniels are used as hunting companions, many are used for all kinds of activities besides field work. They love agility and flyball; some are quite good in obedience, and others are even used as therapy-dogs for children, elderly or ill people. Yet

Welshies are, in general, healthy dogs and can live good long lifespans. Phoebe, pictured second from the right, was 13-and-a-half years old when this photo was taken.

whatever their task in life is, they love doing it and their general attitude is that life is great fun.

It should be remembered that the Welsh Springer Spaniel is a gundog, although he is less used for work nowadays. That doesn't mean, however, that he has lost his working abilities. On the contrary, in many countries people are still training and working their Welshes and although they have to compete against their talented English Springer cousins (often from working lines), they manage to hold their own.

Perhaps the first lines of the poem *Ode to the Welsh Springer Spaniel* by Raynor Jacobs help encapsulate the essence of the breed:

*They asked me what a Welsh
  Springer was:
It's a working dog, I said.
A dog with chestnut, fox-bright
  coat
With Lhanharan spot on head.
A dog with trimming brilliant
  white
And tail quite short, and merry.
A dog to love, and love me too
And bark when necessary.*

BREED-SPECIFIC HEALTH CONSIDERATIONS

Although the Welsh Springer Spaniel is a healthy breed, there are a few breed-related hereditary conditions. Responsible breeders will have their stock examined for these conditions and will not breed from affected stock.

Hip dysplasia is a degeneration of the hip socket into which the femoral head rests. It is common in most breeds of purebred dogs and most breeders x-ray their breeding stock to avoid breeding from affected dogs. In many countries the x-raying is obligatory if you want to breed and results are often published in the club's newsletters and magazines.

Epilepsy is a condition that is caused by a recessive gene; it is very hard to breed it out. Breeders will certainly not breed from affected stock and be very careful in using close relatives of affected dogs for breeding.

Eye diseases include hereditary cataract and goniodysgenesis. Cataract is a condition whereby the lens will become covered with a milky film. It is often seen in older dogs (ten years and older). Since ageing is a gradual process, it is not much cause for concern when a cataract begins to form. However, hereditary cataract is a non-congenital defect and can occur at an early age, affecting the eyesight of the dog; therefore, it is much more serious.

Goniodysgenesis is the predisposing abnormality to primary angle-closure glaucoma. It is a congenital defect.

The Breed Standard for the
WELSH SPRINGER SPANIEL

A stamp issued by the Central African Republic that honours the *Springer Gallois*—the Welsh Springer Spaniel.

The first breed standard was written and officially approved by the Kennel Club in Great Britain in 1902. In later years some minor changes have been made, but on the whole the standard has remained practically unaltered; the latest printed standard dates from 1987. This standard is also officially recognised in all of the FCI (Fédération Cynologique Internationale) countries. The FCI includes the kennel clubs in the following countries: nearly all the continental European countries, Argentina, Brazil, Chile, Colombia, Ecuador, Mexico, Panama, Paraguay, Peru, Puerto Rico, Dominican Republique, Uruguay, Venezuela, Israel, Morocco, South Korea, Japan, Philippines and Thailand. There are several other countries which are not affiliated with the FCI, but associated, such as Bulgaria, Cyprus, Greece, Romania, San Marino, Bermuda, Bolivia, Costa Rica, Cuba, Guatemala, Honduras, Ireland, Hong Kong, India, Indonesia, Malaysia, Singapore, Sri Lanka, Taiwan, Madagascar, South Africa, Zimbabwe, Australia and New Zealand. In these countries the British Standard is the official breed standard. The breed standard as approved by the American Kennel Club is hardly different but certainly more extensive than the British.

THE KENNEL CLUB BREED STANDARD FOR THE WELSH SPRINGER SPANIEL

General Appearance: Symmetrical, compact, not leggy, obviously built for endurance and hard work. Quick and active mover, displaying plenty of push and drive.

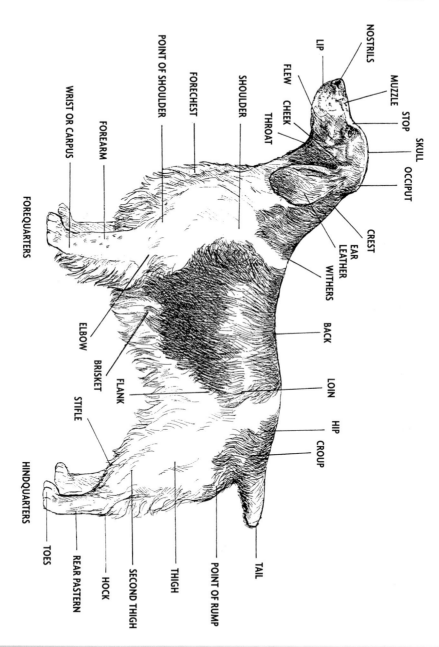

NOSTRILS

LIP

FLEW

MUZZLE

CHEEK

STOP

THROAT

SKULL

OCCIPUT

POINT OF SHOULDER

FORECHEST

SHOULDER

CREST

EAR
LEATHER

WITHERS

WRIST OR CARPUS

FOREARM

BACK

FOREQUARTERS

ELBOW

LOIN

BRISKET

HIP

FLANK

CROUP

STIFLE

HINDQUARTERS

TOES

REAR PASTERN

HOCK

SECOND THIGH

THIGH

POINT OF RUMP

TAIL

Physical Structure of the Welsh Springer Spaniel

Characteristics: Very ancient and distinct breed of pure origin. Strong, merry and very active.

Head and Skull: Skull of proportionate length, slightly domed, clearly defined stop, well chiselled below eyes. Muzzle of medium length, straight, fairly square. Nostrils well developed, flesh coloured to dark.

Eyes: Hazel or dark, medium size, neither prominent, or sunken, or showing haw.

Mouth: Jaws strong with a perfect, regular and complete scissor bite, i.e. upper teeth closely overlapping the lower teeth and set square to the jaws.

LEATHERS

The term 'leathers' refers to the ears of the Welsh Springer Spaniel.

Ears: Set moderately low and hanging close to cheeks. Comparatively small and gradually narrowing towards tip and shaped somewhat like a vine leaf.

Neck: Long, muscular, clean in throat, neatly set into sloping shoulders.

Forequarters: Forelegs of medium length, straight, well boned.

Body: Not long, strong and muscular. Length of body should

Sh Ch Dalati Digwydd is a beautiful example of what a Welsh Springer Spaniel should look like.

be proportionate to length of legs. Loin muscular and slightly arched. Well coupled.

Tail: Well set on and low, never carried above level of back, customarily docked. Lively in action.

Hindquarters: Strong and muscular, wide and fully developed. Hindlegs well boned, hocks well let down, stifles moderately angled, neither turning in nor out.

Feet: Round, with thick pads. Firm and cat-like, not large or spreading.

Gait/Movement: Smooth, powerful, ground covering action; driving from rear.

Coat: Straight or flat, silky texture, dense, never wiry or wavy. Curly coat highly undesirable. Forelegs and hindlegs above hocks moderately feathered, ears and tail lightly feathered.

Colour: Rich red and white only.

Size: Approximate height: dogs 48 cm (19 ins) at withers; bitches 46 cm (18 ins) at withers.

Faults: Any departure from the foregoing points should be considered a fault and the seriousness with which the fault should be

LHANHARAN SPOT
The lozenge-shaped red spot so often found on top of the head between the ears is traditionally called the Lhanharan spot because Colonel Blandy-Jenkins' Lhanharan Welsh Springer Spaniels often had a spot like that.

regarded should be in exact proportion to its degree.

Note: Male animals should have two apparently normal testicles fully descended into the scrotum.

DISTINGUISHABLE TOPLINE
His topline distinguishes the Welsh Springer Spaniel from all the other spaniel varieties.

Your Puppy
WELSH SPRINGER SPANIEL

FINDING A BREEDER

If, after all the information you have amassed about the breed, you are quite sure that you definitely want a Welsh Springer Spaniel, you have to ask yourself if you can give a Welsh Springer the life he needs.

Will you be able to give him all the exercise he requires? Are you willing to spend time with him just playing or sharing activities such as agility or fly ball? Are you prepared to train him for work and can you take him on a shoot?

Whatever you are going to do with him, you will have to give him basic obedience training and you may have to go to classes to do so.

Bearing in mind the difference in temperament you may encounter, have you decided which temperament suits you best?

If you have thought all this out and still believe that a Welsh Springer Spaniel is for you, then your next step is to find a reputable breeder.

It may help you to visit a couple of dog shows or the breed club championship show. Watch the breeders and how they communicate with their dogs.

Look at the dogs and see which breeder has dogs with the type and temperament you like. You can also contact the breed club and ask for names and addresses of breeders with puppies for sale. The club will give you a list of breeders who have puppies that fulfil the club rules. These rules mainly concern matters of hereditary defects in both parents. If the breeders whose dogs you like are not on the list, do not hesitate to contact them and ask if they will have puppies in the future and whether these puppies will fulfil the club rules. If you visit a breeder and you are a bit doubtful about the puppies, the breeder or the conditions in which the puppies are kept, or if the breeder thinks that checking for hereditary defects is not necessary, do not buy the puppy! It must be a 100-percent decision—buying because you are afraid to say no or because you feel sorry for the pup is wrong. After all, you are going to buy a companion for the next 12 to 14 years and you must be absolutely sure that he is the one you want and no other!

Should you want to buy a puppy for showing, discuss this with the breeder. The same goes for working abilities. Also discuss with him what to do in case the puppy will not be showable. Unforeseen changes may happen as the pup grows, such as a mouth that goes wrong. If it is a male, he may turn out to be monorchid (only one descended testicle) etc. If you are very determined to have a show-quality pup, you might do better to buy a more mature puppy, say 6 to 7 months old, so that these risks cannot occur.

Nowadays puppies are often sold with a sales contract. This is fine, but do not sign on the spot. Ask the breeder if you can take it home to read it carefully so that you know exactly what you are going to sign. More important than a sales contract, however, is a good relationship between you and the breeder. A responsible, dedicated breeder is at all times willing to answer all your questions, to calm your fears and to share your joys.

SELECTING A PUPPY

You have found the breeder who has the type of Welsh Springer

A proud mother and her litter. These pups will not be ready to go to new homes until they are at least eight weeks old.

you like and you feel you can trust him. He lets you know he has a litter and there you are, surrounded by all these lovely puppies. How will you ever be able to choose! It is very tempting to let one of them

PUPPY SELECTION

Your selection of a good puppy can be determined by your needs. A show potential or a good pet? It is your choice. Every puppy, however, should be of good temperament. Although show-quality puppies are bred and raised with emphasis on physical conformation, responsible breeders strive for equally good temperament. Do not buy from a breeder who concentrates solely on physical beauty at the expense of personality.

choose you, but remember that this is not the safest approach. Try to make your choice by a process of elimination. If you have decided you want a bitch puppy, ask the breeder to take the dog puppies away, that makes it a bit easier. The litter usually contains a range of temperaments from the boisterous and bossy to the very shy and submissive. Novice dog owners are best advised to choose a puppy of middling nature. Harden your heart and don't go for the nervous and shy ones and ask the breeder to take the shy and bossy puppies away. Now what you are looking for is a healthy, good looking, happy little thing that when you crouch down will in no time be all over you, thinking you are great fun. Ask the breeder if you can see the dam (and sire if possible) and see what her temperament is like. Discuss the pedigree with him, so that you can make sure that your puppy comes from good stock.

A 10-week-old Welsh Springer puppy should have a balanced head with a well-defined stop, a good reach of neck, good ribs and good, well-boned quarters with hocks well let down. Shoulders should be laid back, front legs straight. The feet should be catlike with thick pads. The set of the tail should be a little below the level of the back and it should be carried straight with lively action. The puppy should have nice hazel or dark eyes. A good shiny coat is an indication of good health as is a happy and exuberant temperament. The colour should be a rich red and white.

There is a useful basic checklist for your new puppy:
- check that the puppy is alert and responsive to sounds
- ensure that the puppy has no discharge from the eyes or nose
- check for sores, bald patches or scabs
- check the puppy's stomach—if distended, it could indicate the wrong diet or worms
- check for signs of illness such as coughing
- check that the puppy looks well on the day of collection— if not, arrange to return later
- ask the breeder when the puppy was last wormed and when it should be wormed again.
- ask the breeder about the inoculation program
- check whether the breeder would be willing to take the puppy back should this be necessary

It may seem a lot of effort and it will be very difficult to withstand all those appealing little spaniel faces, but you have to remember that you cannot be too careful when it comes to deciding on the type of dog you

PUPPY APPEARANCE
Your puppy should have a well-fed appearance but not a distended abdomen, which may indicate worms or incorrect feeding, or both. The body should be firm, with a solid feel. The skin of the abdomen should be pale pink and clean, without signs of scratching or rash. Check the hind legs to make certain that dewclaws were removed, if any were present at birth.

want and finding out about your prospective pup's background. Buying a puppy is not—or should not be—just another whimsical purchase. In fact, this is one instance in which you actually do get to choose your own family! But, you may be thinking, buying a puppy should be fun—it should not be so serious and so much work. If you

DID YOU KNOW?

Breeders rarely release puppies until they are eight to ten weeks of age. This is an acceptable age for most breeds of dog, excepting toy breeds, which are not released until around 12 weeks, given their petite sizes. If a breeder has a puppy that is 12 weeks or more, it is likely well socialised and housetrained. Be sure that it is otherwise healthy before deciding to take it home.

keep in mind the thought that your puppy is not a cuddly stuffed toy or decorative lawn ornament, but instead will become a real member of your family, you will realise that while buying a puppy is a pleasurable and exciting endeavour, it is not something to be taken lightly.

Two adorable three-week-old Welshie pups.

Relax…the fun will start when the pup comes home!

Always keep in mind that a puppy is nothing more than a baby in a furry disguise…a baby who is virtually helpless in a human world and who trusts his owner for fulfilment of his basic needs for survival. That goes beyond food, water and shelter; your pup needs care, protection, guidance and love. If you are not prepared to commit to this, then you are not prepared to own a dog.

Do not worry too much about it though; you will probably find that once your pup gets used to his new home, he will fall into his place in the family quite naturally. But it never hurts to emphasise the commitment of dog ownership. With some time and patience, it is really not too difficult to raise a curious and exuberant Springer Spaniel pup to be a well-adjusted and well-mannered adult dog—a dog that could be your most loyal friend.

BOY OR GIRL?

An important consideration to be discussed is the sex of your puppy. For a family companion, a bitch may be the better choice, considering the female's inbred concern for all young creatures and her accompanying tolerance and patience. It is always advisable to spay a pet bitch, which may guarantee her a longer life.

PREPARING PUPPY'S PLACE IN YOUR HOME

Researching your breed and finding a breeder are only two aspects of the 'homework' you will have to do before bringing your puppy home. You will also have to prepare your home and family for the new addition. Just as you would prepare a nursery for a newborn baby, you will need to designate a place in your home that will be the puppy's own. How you prepare your home will depend on how much freedom the dog will be allowed: will he be confined to one room or a specific area in the house, or will he be allowed to roam as he pleases? Will he spend most of his time in the house or will he be primarily an outdoor dog? Whatever you decide, you must ensure that he has a place that he

PREPARING FOR PUP

Unfortunately, when a puppy is bought by someone who does not take into consideration the time and attention that dog ownership requires, it is the puppy who suffers when he is either abandoned or placed in a shelter by a frustrated owner. So all of the 'homework' you do in preparation for your pup's arrival will benefit you both. The more informed you are, the more you will know what to expect and the better equipped you will be to handle the ups and downs of raising a puppy. Hopefully, everyone in the household is willing to do his part in raising and caring for the pup. The anticipation of owning a dog often brings a lot of promises from excited family members: 'I will walk him every day,' 'I will feed him,' 'I will housebreak him,' etc., but these things take time and effort, and promises can easily be forgotten once the novelty of the new pet has worn off.

INSURANCE

Many good breeders will offer you insurance with your new puppy, which is an excellent idea. The first few weeks of insurance will probably be covered free of charge or with only minimal cost, allowing you to take up the policy when this expires. If you own a pet dog, it is sensible to take out such a policy as veterinary fees can be high, although routine vaccinations and boosters are not covered. Look carefully at the many options open to you before deciding which suits you best.

A tiny newborn Welsh Springer Spaniel.

can 'call his own.'

When you bring your new puppy into your home, you are bringing him into what will become his home as well. Obviously, you did not buy a puppy so that he could take over your house, but in order for a puppy to grow into a stable, well-

DOCUMENTATION

Two important documents you will get from the breeder are the pup's pedigree and registration certificate. The breeder should register the litter and each pup with The Kennel Club, and it is necessary for you to have the paperwork if you plan on showing or breeding in the future.

Make sure you know the breeder's intentions on which type of registration he will obtain for the pup. There are limited registrations which may prohibit the dog from being shown, bred or from competing in non-conformation trials such as Working or Agility if the breeder feels that the pup is not of sufficient quality to do so. There is also a type of registration that will permit the dog in non-conformation competition only.

On the reverse side of the registration certificate, the new owner can find the transfer section which must be signed by the breeder.

YOUR SCHEDULE . . .

If you lead an erratic, unpredictable life, with daily or weekly changes in your work requirements, consider the problems of owning a puppy. The new puppy has to be fed regularly, socialised (loved, petted, handled, introduced to other people) and, most importantly, allowed to visit outdoors for toilet training. As the dog gets older, it can be more tolerant of deviations in its feeding and toilet relief.

adjusted dog, he has to feel comfortable in his surroundings. Remember, he is leaving the warmth and security of his mother and littermates, plus the familiarity of the only place he has ever known, so it is important to make his transition as easy as possible. By preparing a place in your home for the puppy, you are making him feel as welcome as possible in a strange new place. It should not take him long to get used to it, but the sudden shock of being transplanted is somewhat traumatic for a young pup. Imagine how a small child would feel in the same situation—that is how your puppy must be feeling. It is up to you to reassure him and to let him know, 'Little chap, you are going to like it here!'

WHAT YOU SHOULD BUY

CRATE

To someone unfamiliar with the use of crates in dog training, it may seem like punishment to shut a dog in a crate; this is not the case at all. Crates are not cruel—crates have many humane and highly effective uses in dog care and training. For example, crate training is a very popular and very successful

ARE YOU A FIT OWNER?
If the breeder from whom you are buying a puppy asks you a lot of personal questions, do not be insulted. Such a breeder wants to be sure that you will be a fit provider for his puppy.

QUALITY FOOD
The cost of food must also be mentioned. All dogs need a good quality food with an adequate supply of protein to develop their bones and muscles properly. Most dogs are not picky eaters but unless fed properly they can quickly succumb to skin problems.

housebreaking method; a crate can keep your dog safe during travel; and, perhaps most importantly, a crate provides your dog with a place of his own in your home. It serves as a 'doggie bedroom' of sorts—your Welsh can curl up in his crate when he wants to sleep or when he just needs a break. Many dogs sleep in their crates overnight. When lined with soft blankets and filled with his favourite toys and stuffed pals, a crate becomes a cosy pseudo-den for your dog. Like his ancestors, he too will seek out the comfort and retreat of a den—you just happen to be providing him with something a

Your local pet shop will have a selection of crates from which you can find the one that best suits your needs.

PHOTO COURTESY OF DOSKOCIL

dog. The size of the crate is another thing to consider. Puppies do not stay puppies forever—in fact, sometimes it seems as if they grow right before your eyes. Unless you have the money and the inclination to buy a new crate every time your pup has a growth spurt, it is better to get one that will accommodate your dog both as a pup and at full size. The proper size crate will allow the adult Springer to stand up and lie down.

BEDDING

A blanket or, ideally, a vetbed, in the dog's crate will help the dog feel more at home. Either will take the place of the leaves, twigs, etc., that the pup would use in the wild to make a den; the pup can make his own 'burrow' in the crate. Although your pup is far removed from his den-making ancestors, the denning instinct is still a part of his genetic makeup. Second, until you bring your pup home, he has been sleeping amidst the warmth of his mother and litter-mates, and while a blanket is not the same as a warm, breathing body, it still provides heat and something with which to snuggle. You will want to wash your pup's bedding frequently in case he has an accident in his crate, and replace or remove any blanket that becomes ragged and starts to fall apart.

little more luxurious than leaves and twigs lining a dirty ditch.

As far as purchasing a crate, the type that you buy is up to you. It will most likely be one of the two most popular types: wire or fibreglass. There are advantages and disadvantages to each type. For example, a wire crate is more open, allowing the air to flow through and affording the dog a view of what is going on around him. A fibreglass crate, however, is sturdier and can double as a travel crate since it provides more protection for the

Toys

Toys are a must for dogs of all ages, especially for curious playful pups. Puppies are the 'children' of the dog world, and what child does not love toys? Chew toys provide enjoyment to both dog and owner—your dog will enjoy playing with his favourite toys, while you will enjoy the fact that they distract him from your expensive shoes and leather sofa. Welshes can be chewers, especially while teething. In fact, chewing is a physical need for all pups as they are teething, and everything looks appetising! The full range of your possessions— from old tea towel to Oriental carpet—are fair game in the eyes of a teething pup. Puppies are not all that discerning when it comes to finding something to literally 'sink their teeth into'—everything tastes great!

Stuffed toys are another option; these are good to put in the dog's crate to give him some company. Be careful of these, as a pup can de-stuff one pretty quickly, and stay away from stuffed toys with small plastic eyes or parts that a pup could choke on. Similarly, squeaky toys are quite popular. There are dogs that will come running from anywhere in the house at the first sound from their favourite squeaky friend. Again, if a pup de-stuffs one of these, the small plastic squeaker inside can be dangerous if swallowed. Monitor the condition of your pup's toys carefully and get rid of any that have been chewed to the point of becoming potentially dangerous.

Be careful of natural bones, which have a tendency to splinter into sharp, dangerous pieces.

CRATE TRAINING TIPS

During crate training, you should partition off the section of the crate in which the pup stays. If he is given too big an area, this will hinder your training efforts. Crate training is based on the fact that a dog does not like to soil his sleeping quarters, so it is ineffective to keep a pup in a crate that is so big that he can eliminate in one end and get far enough away from it to sleep. Also, you want to make the crate den-like for the pup. Blankets and a favourite toy will make the crate cosy for the small pup; as he grows, you may want to evict some of his 'roommates' to make more room.

It will take some coaxing at first, but be patient. Given some time to get used to it, your pup will adapt to his new home-within-a-home quite nicely.

TOYS, TOYS, TOYS!

With a big variety of dog toys available, and so many that look like they would be a lot of fun for a dog, be careful in your selection. It is amazing what a set of puppy teeth can do to an innocent-looking toy, so, obviously, safety is a major consideration. Be sure to choose the most durable products that you can find. Hard nylon bones and toys are a safe bet, and many of them are offered in different scents and flavours that will be sure to capture your dog's attention. It is always fun to play a game of catch with your dog, and there are balls and flying discs that are specially made to withstand dog teeth.

Select a lead made from a durable material that is not too heavy. Nylon is a good choice for the Welsh Springer Spaniel.

Also be careful of rawhide, which after enough chewing can turn into pieces that are easy to swallow, and also watch out for the mushy mess it can become on your carpet. Most puppies love calf hooves which you can buy in any pet shop or at shows. They can chew for hours on them without coming to any harm. However, if what's left of the hoof becomes too small, you are advised to dispose of it.

LEAD

A nylon lead is probably the best option as it is the most resistant to puppy teeth should your pup take a liking to chewing on his lead. Of course, this is a habit that should be nipped in the bud, but if your pup likes to chew on

his lead he has a very slim chance of being able to chew through the strong nylon. Nylon leads are also lightweight, which is good for a young Springer puppy who is just getting used to the idea of walking on a lead. For everyday walking and safety purposes, the nylon lead is a good choice. As your pup grows up and gets used to walking on the lead, and can do it politely, you may want to purchase a flexible lead, which allows you either to extend the length to give the dog a broader area to explore or to pull in the lead when you want to keep him close.

COLLAR

Your pup should get used to wearing a collar because the lead and collar go hand in hand—you have to attach the lead to something! A lightweight nylon collar will be a good choice; make sure that it fits snugly enough so that the pup cannot wriggle out of it, but loose enough so that it will not be uncomfortably tight around the pup's neck. You should be able to fit a finger in between the pup and the collar. It may take some time for your pup to get used to wearing the collar, but soon he will not even notice that it is there. Choke collars are made for training, but should only be used by an owner who knows exactly how to use it.

> ### FINANCIAL RESPONSIBILITY
> Grooming tools, collars, leashes, dog beds and, of course, toys will be an expense to you when you first obtain your pup, and the cost will continue throughout your dog's lifetime. If your puppy damages or destroys your possessions (as most puppies surely will!) or something belonging to a neighbour, you can calculate additional expense. There is also flea and pest control, which every dog owner faces more than once. You must be able to handle the financial responsibility of owning a dog.

FOOD AND WATER BOWLS

Your pup will need two bowls, one for food and one for water. You may want two sets of bowls, one for inside and one for outside, depending on where the dog will be fed and where he will be spending most of his time. Stainless steel bowl are good but the sturdy special spaniel bowls whose shape allows the ears to fall outside the bowl are popular choices. These bowls save you messy ears after food consump-

Purchase sturdy food and water bowls for your Welshie... stainless steel, heavy plastic and crockery are popular choices.

PHOTO COURTESY OF MIKKI PET PRODUCTS.

tion and a wet floor after drinking! Plastic bowls are very chewable and therefore not advisable. Some dog owners like to put their dogs' food and water bowls on a specially made elevated stand; this brings the food closer to the dog's level so he does not have to bend down as far, thus aiding his digestion and helping to guard against bloat or gastric torsion in deep-chested dogs. The most important thing is to buy sturdy bowls since, again, anything is in danger of being chewed by puppy teeth and you do not want your dog to be constantly chewing apart his bowl (for his safety and for your wallet!).

CLEANING SUPPLIES

A pup that is not housetrained means you will be doing a lot of cleaning until he is. Accidents will occur, which is okay for now because he does not know any better. All you can do is clean up any 'accidents'—old rags, towels, newspapers and a safe disinfectant are good to have on hand.

BEYOND THE BASICS

The items previously discussed are the bare necessities. You will find out what else you need as you go along—grooming supplies, flea/tick protection, baby gates to partition a room, etc.—these things will vary depending on your situation. It is

CHOOSE AN APPROPRIATE COLLAR

The **BUCKLE COLLAR** is the standard collar used for everyday purpose. Be sure that you adjust the buckle on growing puppies. Check it every day. It can become too tight overnight! These collars can be made of leather or nylon. Attach your dog's identification tags to this collar.

The **CHOKE COLLAR** is the usual collar recommended for training. It is constructed of highly polished steel so that it slides easily through the stainless steel loop. The idea is that the dog controls the pressure around its neck and he will stop pulling if the collar becomes uncomfortable. Never leave a choke collar on your dog when not training.

The **HALTER** is for a trained dog that has to be restrained to prevent running away, chasing a cat and the like. Considered the most humane of all collars, it is frequently used on smaller dogs for which collars are not comfortable.

You should always clean up after your Welsh Springer Spaniel regardless of where he relieves himself. You can purchase a device to help you with this task.

just important that right away you have everything you need to feed and make your new family member comfortable in his first few days at home.

PUPPY-PROOFING YOUR HOME

Aside from making sure that your puppy will be comfortable in your home, you also have to make sure that your home is safe for your pup. This means taking precautions to ensure that your pup will not get into anything he should not get into and that there is nothing within his reach that

may harm him should he sniff it, chew it, inspect it, etc. This probably seems obvious since, while you are primarily concerned with your pup's safety, at the same time you do not want your belongings to be ruined. Breakables should be placed out of reach if your dog is to have full run of the house. If he is to be limited to certain places within the house, keep any potentially dangerous items in the 'off-limits' areas. An electrical cord can pose a danger should the puppy decide to taste it—and who is going to convince a pup that it would not make a great chew toy? Cords should be placed under the carpeting or fastened tightly against the wall. If your dog is going to spend time in a crate, make sure that there is nothing near his crate that he can reach if he sticks his curious little nose or paws through the openings. And just as you would with a child, keep all household cleaners and chemicals where the

PUPPY-PROOFING

Thoroughly puppy-proof your house before bringing your puppy home. Never use roach or rodent poisons in any area accessible to the puppy. Avoid the use of toilet cleaners. Most dogs are born with 'toilet sonar' and will take a drink if the lid is left open. Also keep the rubbish secured and out of reach.

pup cannot get to them.

It is just as important to make sure that the outside of your home is safe. Of course your puppy should never be unsupervised, but a pup let loose in the garden will want to run and explore, and he should be granted that freedom. Do not let a fence give you a false sense of security; you would be surprised how crafty (and persistent) a dog can be in figuring out how to dig under and squeeze his way through small holes, or to jump or climb over a fence. The remedy is to make the fence high enough so that it really is impossible for your dog to get over it (about 3 metres should suffice), and well embedded into the ground. Be sure to repair or secure any gaps in the fence. Check the fence periodically to ensure that it is in good shape and make repairs as needed; a very determined pup may return

NATURAL TOXINS

Examine your grass and garden landscaping before bringing your puppy home. Many varieties of plants have leaves, stems or flowers that are toxic if ingested, and you can depend on a curious puppy to investigate them. Ask your vet for information on poisonous plants or research them at your library.

CHEMICAL TOXINS

Scour your garage for potential puppy dangers. Remove weed killers, pesticides and antifreeze materials. Antifreeze is highly toxic and even a few drops can kill an adult dog. The sweet taste attracts the animal, who will quickly consume it from the floor or curbside.

to the same spot to 'work on it' until he is able to get through.

FIRST TRIP TO THE VET

So, you have picked out your puppy, your home and family are ready, now all you have to do is pick your Springer up from the breeder and the fun begins, right? Well…not so fast. Something else you need to prepare for is your pup's first trip to the veterinary surgeon. Perhaps the breeder can recommend someone in the area or maybe some other dog-owners can suggest a good vet. Either way, you should have an appointment arranged for your pup before you pick him up; plan on taking him for a checkup within the first few days of bringing him home.

The pup's first visit will consist of an overall examination to make sure that the pup does not have any problems that are not apparent to the eye. The veterinary surgeon will also set up a schedule for the pup's vaccinations; the breeder will inform you of which ones the pup has already received and the vet can continue from there.

INTRODUCTION TO THE FAMILY

Everyone in the house will be excited about the puppy coming home and will want to pet him and play with him, but it is best to make the introduction low-key so as not to overwhelm the puppy. He is apprehensive already; it is the first time he has been separated from his mother and the breeder, and the ride to your home is likely the first time he has been in a car. The last thing you want to do is smother him, as this will only frighten him further. This is not to say that human contact is not extremely necessary at this stage, because this is the time

Having your puppy examined by the veterinary surgeon and keeping current on the pup's vaccinations are absolute necessities.

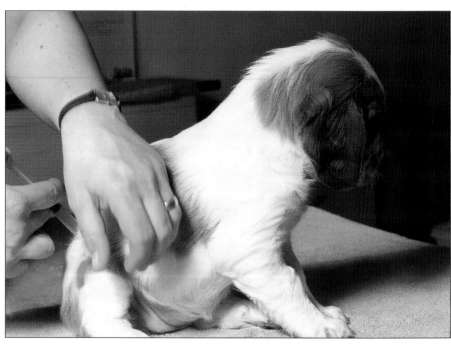

when an instant connection between the pup and his human family is formed. Gentle petting and soothing words should help console him, as well as just putting him down and letting him explore on his own (under your watchful eye, of course).

The pup may approach the family members or may busy himself with exploring for a while. Gradually, each person should spend some time with the pup, one at a time, crouching down to get as close to the pup's level as possible and letting him sniff their hands and petting him gently. He definitely needs human attention and he needs to be touched—this is how to form an immediate bond. Just remember that the pup is experiencing many things for

TOXIC PLANTS
Many plants can be toxic to dogs. If you see your dog carrying a piece of vegetation in his mouth, approach him in a quiet, disinterested manner, avoid eye contact, pet him and gradually remove the plant from his mouth. Alternatively, offer him a treat and maybe he'll drop the plant on his own accord. Be sure no toxic plants are growing in your own garden.

the first time, all at the same time. There are new people, new noises, new smells, and new things to investigate; so be gentle, be affectionate and be as comforting as you can be.

YOUR PUP'S FIRST NIGHT HOME
You have travelled home with your new charge safely in his basket or crate. He's been to the vet for a thorough check-up; he's been weighed, his papers examined; perhaps he's even been vaccinated and wormed as

THE TRIP HOME
Taking your dog from the breeder to your home in a car can be a very uncomfortable experience for both of you. The puppy will have been taken from his warm, friendly, safe environment and brought into a strange new environment. An environment that moves! Be prepared for loose bowels, urination, crying, whining and even fear biting. With proper love and encouragement when you arrive home, the stress of the trip should quickly disappear.

A FORTNIGHT'S GRACE
It will take at least two weeks for your puppy to become accustomed to his new surroundings. Give him lots of love, attention, handling, frequent opportunities to relieve himself, a diet he likes to eat and a place he can call his own.

well. He's met the family, licked the whole family, including the excited children and the less-than-happy cat. He's explored his area, his new bed, the garden and anywhere else he's been permitted. He's eaten his first meal at home and relieved himself in the proper place. He's heard lots of new sounds, smelled new friends and seen more of the outside world than ever before.

That was the just the first day! He's exhausted and ready for bed...or so you think!

It's puppy's first night and you are ready to say 'Good night'—keep in mind that this is puppy's first night ever to be sleeping alone. His dam and littermates are no longer at paw's length and he's a bit scared, cold and lonely. Be reassuring to your new family member. This is not the time to spoil him and give in to his inevitable whining.

Puppies whine. They whine to let the others know where they are and hopefully to get company out of it. Place your pup in his new bed or crate in his room and close the door. Mercifully, he will fall asleep without a peep. If the inevitable occurs, ignore the whining; he is fine. Be strong and keep his interest in mind. Do not allow your heart to become guilty and visit the pup. He will fall asleep.

Many breeders recommend placing a piece of bedding from his former home in his new bed so that he recognises the scent of his littermates. Others still advise placing a hot water

STRESS-FREE
Some experts in canine health advise that stress during a dog's early years of development can compromise and weaken his immune system and may trigger the potential for a shortened life expectancy. They emphasise the need for happy and stress-free growing-up years.

HOW VACCINES WORK

If you've just bought a puppy, you surely know the importance of having your pup vaccinated, but do you understand how vaccines work? Vaccines contain the same bacteria or viruses that cause the disease you want to prevent, but they have been chemically modified so that they don't cause any harm. Instead, the vaccine causes your dog to produce antibodies that fight the harmful bacteria. Thus, if your pup is exposed to the disease in the future, the antibodies will destroy the viruses or bacteria.

PREVENTING PUPPY PROBLEMS

SOCIALISATION

Now that you have done all of the preparatory work and have helped your pup get accustomed to his new home and family, it is about time for you to have some fun! Socialising your Springer pup gives you the opportunity to show off your new friend, and your pup gets to reap the benefits of being

FEEDING TIP

You will probably start feeding your pup the same food that he has been getting from the breeder; the breeder should give you a few days' supply to start you off. Although you should not give your pup too many treats, you will want to have puppy treats on hand for coaxing, training, rewards, etc. Be careful, though, as a small pup's calorie requirements are relatively low and a few treats can add up to almost a full day's worth of calories without the required nutrition.

bottle in his bed for warmth. This latter may be a good idea provided the pup doesn't attempt to suckle—he'll get good and wet and may not fall asleep so fast.

Puppy's first night can be somewhat stressful for the pup and his new family. Remember that you are setting the tone of night-time at your house. Unless you want to play with your pup every evening at 10 p.m., midnight and 2 a.m., don't initiate the habit. Surely your family will thank you, and so will your pup!

MANNERS MATTER

During the socialisation process, a puppy should meet people, experience different environments and definitely be exposed to other canines. Through playing and interacting with other dogs, your puppy will learn lessons, ranging from controlling the pressure of his jaws by biting his litter mates to the inner-workings of the canine pack that he will apply to his human relationships for the rest of his life. That is why removing a puppy from its litter too early (before eight weeks) can be detrimental to the pup's development.

animals and situations. This will help him become well adjusted as he grows up and less prone to being timid or fearful of the new things he will encounter. Your pup's socialisation began at the breeder's, now it is your responsibility to continue. The socialisation he receives up until the age of 12 weeks is the most critical, as this is the time when he forms his impressions of the outside world. Lack of socialisation can manifest itself in fear and aggression as the dog grows up. Luckily, Welshes are not dog-aggressive; in fact, they are very friendly, even exuberant, around other dogs. He needs lots of human interaction, affection, handling and exposure to other animals. Be careful during the eight-to-ten-week period, also known as the fear period. The interaction he receives during this time should be gentle and reassuring.

Once your pup has received his necessary vaccinations, feel free to take him out and about (on his lead, of course). Take him around the neighbourhood, take him on your daily errands, let people pet him, let him meet other dogs and pets, etc. Puppies do not have to try to make friends; there will be no shortage of people who will want to introduce themselves. Just make sure that you

an adorable furry creature that people will coo over, want to pet and, in general, think is absolutely precious!

Besides getting to know his new family, your puppy should be exposed to other people, carefully supervise each interaction. If the neighbourhood children want to say hello, for example, that is great—children and pups most often make great companions. But sometimes an excited child can unintentionally handle a pup too roughly, or an overzealous pup can playfully nip a little too hard. You want to make socialisation experiences positive ones; what a pup learns during this very formative stage will affect his attitude toward future encounters. A pup that has a bad experience with a child may grow up to be a dog that is shy around or aggressive toward children, and you want your dog to be comfortable around everyone.

CONSISTENCY IN TRAINING
Dogs, being pack animals, naturally need a leader, or else they try to establish dominance

> ### PROPER SOCIALISATION
> The socialisation period for puppies is from age 8 to 16 weeks. This is the time when puppies need to leave their birth family and take up residence with their new owners, where they will meet many new people, other pets, etc. Failure to be adequately socialised can cause the dog to grow up fearing others and being shy and unfriendly due to a lack of self-confidence.

in their packs. When you bring a dog into your family, who becomes the leader and who becomes the 'pack' are entirely up to you! Your pup's intuitive quest for dominance, coupled with the fact that it is nearly impossible to look at an adorable pup, with his soulful eyes and his long ears, and not cave in, give the pup almost an

> ### SOCIALISATION
> Thorough socialisation includes not only meeting new people but also being introduced to new experiences such as riding in the car, having his coat brushed, hearing the television, walking in a crowd—the list is endless. The more your pup experiences, and the more positive the experiences are, the less of a shock and the less frightening it will be for your pup to encounter new things.

A pup that is destined for the show ring must be socialised to a multitude of experiences—handling by the judge, interaction with other dogs, being in crowds of people, etc. Of course, these are situations in which all dogs, no matter pet or show, should behave properly.

unfair advantage in getting the upper hand! And a pup will definitely test the waters to see

PLAY'S THE THING

Teaching the puppy to play with his toys in running and fetching games is an ideal way to help the puppy develop muscle, learn motor skills and bond with you his owner and master.

He also needs to learn how to inhibit his bite reflex and never to use his teeth on people, forbidden objects and other animals in play. Whenever you play with your puppy, you make the rules. This becomes an important message to your puppy in teaching him that you are the pack leader and control everything he does in life. Once your dog accepts you as his leader, your relationship with him will be cemented for life.

what he can and cannot get away with. Do not give in to those pleading eyes—stand your ground when it comes to disciplining the pup and make sure that all family members do the same. It will only confuse the pup when Mother tells him to get off the couch when he is used to sitting up there with Father to watch the nightly news. Avoid discrepancies by having all members of the household decide on the rules before the pup even comes home…and be consistent in enforcing them! Early training shapes the dog's personality, so you cannot be unclear in what you expect.

COMMON PUPPY PROBLEMS

The best way to prevent problems is to be proactive in stopping an undesirable behaviour as soon as it starts. The old saying 'You can't teach an old dog new tricks' does not necessarily hold true, but it is true that it is much easier to discourage bad behaviour in a young developing pup than to

NO CHOCOLATE!

Use treats to bribe your dog into a desired behaviour. Try small pieces of hard cheese or freeze-dried liver. Never offer chocolate as it has toxic qualities for dogs.

wait until the pup's bad behaviour becomes the adult dog's bad habit. There are some problems that are especially prevalent in puppies as they develop.

NIPPING

As puppies start to teethe, they feel the need to sink their teeth into anything...unfortunately that includes your fingers, arms, hair, toes...whatever happens to be available. You may find this behaviour cute for about the first five seconds...until you feel just how sharp those puppy teeth are. This is something you want to discourage immediately and consistently with a firm 'No!' (or whatever number of firm 'No's' it takes for him to understand that you mean business) and replace your finger with an appropriate chew toy. While this behaviour is merely annoying when the dog is still young, it can become highly unpleasant as your Springer Spaniel's adult teeth grow in and his jaws develop, if he thinks that it is acceptable to gnaw on human appendages.

CRYING/WHINING

Your pup will often cry, whine, whimper, howl or make some type of commotion when he is left alone. This is basically his way of calling out for attention, of calling out to make sure that

TRAINING TIP
Training your puppy takes much patience and can be frustrating at times, but you should see results from your efforts. If you have a puppy that seems untrainable, take him to a trainer or behaviourist. The dog may have a personality problem that requires the help of a professional, or perhaps you need help in learning how to train your dog.

you know he is there and that you have not forgotten about him. He feels insecure when he is left alone, for example, when you are out of the house and he is in his crate or when you are in another part of the house and he cannot see you. The noise he is making is an expression of the anxiety he feels at being alone, so he needs to be taught that being alone is okay. You are not actually training the dog to stop making noise, you are training him to feel comfortable when he is alone and thus removing the need for him to make the noise. This is where the crate filled with cosy blankets and toys comes in handy. You want to know that he is safe when you are not there to supervise, and you know that he will be safe in his crate rather than roaming freely about the house. In order for the pup to stay in his crate without making a fuss, he needs to be comfortable in his crate. On that note, it is extremely important that the crate is never used as a form of punishment, or the pup will have a negative association with the crate.

Accustom the pup to the crate in short, gradually increasing time intervals in which you put him in the crate, maybe with a treat, and stay in the room with him. If he cries or makes a fuss, do not go to him, but stay in his sight. Gradually he will realise that staying in his crate is all right without your help, and it will not be so traumatic for him when you are not around. You may want to leave the radio on softly when you leave the house; the sound of human voices may be comforting to him.

CHEWING TIPS

Chewing goes hand in hand with nipping in the sense that a teething puppy is always looking for a way to soothe his aching gums. In this case, instead of chewing on you, he may have taken a liking to your favourite shoe or something else which he should not be chewing. Again, realise that this is a normal canine behaviour that does not need to be discouraged, only redirected. Your pup just needs to be taught what is acceptable to chew on and what is off limits. Consistently tell him NO when you catch him chewing on something forbidden and give him a chew toy. Conversely, praise him when you catch him chewing on something appropriate. In this way you are discouraging the inappropriate behaviour and reinforcing the desired behaviour. The puppy chewing should stop after his adult teeth have come in, but an adult dog continues to chew for various reasons—perhaps because he is bored, perhaps to relieve tension or perhaps he just likes to chew. That is why it is important to redirect his chewing when he is still young.

FEEDING

The health of your dog is mainly dependent on what you feed him. Therefore it is of the utmost importance to select the food that suits him best. Factors to be considered are his age, his condition and his activities; is he a puppy or an adult, is he too thin or too fat and is he an active working dog or just a pet?

Although there are dozens of brands, there are four basic types of dog food: fresh, preferably raw meat, dried food, semi-moist food and canned or tinned meat. For meat the most commonly used is tripe and dogs love it. You can combine their meat meals with dried food or with a semi-moist meal or if fresh meat is not available, with canned meat. Dried foods are less expensive but dogs often get bored with them. How would you feel if you had the same meal day after day, year after year? Most dogs love vegetables and fruit and it certainly doesn't do them any harm to surprise them with a quarter of an apple, some leftover runner beans or lettuce.

When selecting your dog's diet, three stages of development must be considered: the puppy stage, adult stage and the senior or veteran stage.

PUPPY STAGE

A most moving and wondrous sight occurs when the newborn puppy, still wet, blind and deaf and unable to walk knows within minutes to find its way

> **FEEDING TIP**
> You must store your dried dog food carefully. Open packages of dog food quickly lose their vitamin value, usually within 90 days of being opened. Mould spores and vermin could also contaminate the food.

A litter of seven will certainly keep a mother busy! The pups are getting proper nutrition from their mother's milk, but a nursing bitch may have special dietary needs for which the vet should be consulted.

to its mother's teats. The time a breeder cherishes is when the litter has been born and all the puppies are sucking enthusiastically with their tired but very contented mum who is still busy cleaning and drying them. Those first moment of drinking are very important because this early milk contains colostrum which helps to protect the puppies during the first five to six weeks of their lives. Although there are many excellent milk products available, there is nothing as good as a mother's milk and should the mother for some reason not have sufficient milk

or be unable to feed the pups, it is of the utmost importance that you seek the help of your vet to advise you what quality and quantity of milk to feed the puppies. In that case there is lot of work lying ahead of you. Not only do the puppies have to be

TEST FOR PROPER DIET
A good test for proper diet is the colour, odour and firmness of your dog's stool. A healthy dog usually produces three semi-hard stools per day. The stools should have no unpleasant odour. They should be the same colour from excretion to excretion.

fed every two hours around the clock, but you will also have to massage them after each feed to stimulate their digestion and to have them produce stools.

Depending on the size of the litter and the quantity of milk the mother has, you start weaning the puppies at two to three weeks. You can begin with small portions of suitable solid food. Most breeders like to start with minced meat and a couple of days later with some milky food. Gradually the quantities and the number of meals are increased until six weeks old when the pups do not really need mum any more. Selection of the most suitable, good-quality diet at this time is essential, for a puppy's fastest growth rate is during the first year of its life. Veterinary surgeons or other, experienced breeders are able to offer you good advice in this regard. The frequency of meals will have to be reduced over time and by the time the dog is 18 months he can be fed an adult diet.

Puppy Diets

Puppy and junior diets should be well balanced for the needs of your dog, so that except in certain circumstances additional vitamins, minerals and proteins will not be required.

When you decided to buy

FOOD PREFERENCE

Selecting the best dried dog food is difficult. There is no majority consensus among veterinary scientists as to the value of nutrient analyses (protein, fat, fibre, moisture, ash, cholesterol, minerals, etc.). All agree that feeding trials are what matters, but you also have to consider the individual dog. Its weight, age, activity and what pleases its taste, all must be considered. It is probably best to take the advice of your veterinary surgeon. Every dog's dietary requirements vary, even during the lifetime of a particular dog.

If your dog is fed a good dried food, it does not require supplements of meat or vegetables. Dogs do appreciate a little variety in their diets so you may choose to stay with the same brand, but vary the flavour. Alternatively you may wish to add a little flavoured stock to give a difference to the taste.

GRAIN-BASED DIETS

Some less expensive dog foods are based on grains and other plant proteins. While these products may appear to be attractively priced, many breeders prefer a diet based on animal proteins and believe that they are more conducive to your dog's health. Many grain-based diets rely on soy protein that may cause flatulence (passing gas).

There are many cases, however, when your dog might require a special diet. These special requirements should only be recommended by your veterinary surgeon.

your puppy the breeder probably told you what you had to feed the puppy once you brought him home. If he didn't, ask him. This is important for two reasons: coming to live in totally new surroundings with so many new experiences is already a stressful experience for the puppy and a continuation of his diet will help him. Even then his tummy may be upset the first couple of days, or he may even refuse to eat for a day or two, but don't worry about that. As soon as he is settled down he will eat again, especially if it's the food he has been used to. Also, the breeder most likely has a lot of experience in feeding mature dogs and puppies and keeping them in a peak condition, so it would be wise to listen to his advice. Most breeders will provide you with an exact list what to feed the puppy at which stage of his life and we strongly advise you to follow these instructions. Once your puppy is a mature one or two year old, you can change his diet to what is more convenient for you (availability, costs, etc.), but with the growing puppy and youngster, stick to the breeder's diet. And remember that if ten breeders are discussing the feeding of their dogs, you will hear ten different opinions, and all of them will be right!

Your puppy will need three or four meals a day until he is about nine months old, then you can cut back to two daily meals. Some people prefer to feed the adult dog once a day but if your dog loves his food, he probably won't go along with that! He might prefer to have a breakfast and a dinner. Sometimes a Welsh Springer can be a finicky eater. Don't make the mistake in trying to find out what he would like to eat, because that will most certainly worsen the problem. Give him the food you want him to eat and if he doesn't eat it, take it away. Let him be hungry for some hours and you will find that next time you feed him he will attack his foodbowl with more enthusiasm. It is important though, that when is eating badly, the food he does eat is of the highest qualilty. Welshes can be bad eaters until they are eighteen to twenty-four months old and they remain very thin for a long time. Don't despair: They will eat and within a couple of years you have to be careful that he is not growing too fat!

ADULT DIETS

A dog is considered an adult when it has stopped growing. The growth is in height and/or length. Do not consider the

FEEDING TIP

Dog food must be at room temperature, neither too hot nor too cold. Fresh water, changed daily and served in a clean bowl, is mandatory, especially when feeding dried food.

Never feed your dog from the table while you are eating. Never feed your dog leftovers from your own meal. They usually contain too much fat and too much seasoning.

Dogs must chew their food. Hard pellets are excellent; soups and slurries are to be avoided.

Don't add left-overs or any extras to normal dog food. The normal food is usually balanced and adding something extra destroys the balance.

Except for age-related changes, dogs do not require dietary variations. They can be fed the same diet, day after day, without their becoming ill.

TIPPING THE SCALES

Good nutrition is vital to your dog's health, but many people end up over-feeding or giving unnecessary supplements. Here are some common doggie diet don'ts:

• Adding milk, yoghurt and cheese to your dog's diet may seem like a good idea for coat and skin care, but dairy products are very fattening and can cause indigestion.

• Diets high in fat will not cause heart attacks in dogs but will certainly cause your dog to gain weight.

• Most importantly, don't assume your dog will simply stop eating once he doesn't need any more food. Given the chance, he will eat you out of house and home!

dog's weight when the decision is made to switch from a puppy diet to a maintenance diet. Again you should rely on your breeder's advice. A Welsh Springer Spaniel reaches adulthood at about 2-1/2 to 3-1/2 years of age, though some dogs are fully mature at two years of age while others look their best when they are four.

Whatever you are going to feed your dog don't rely entirely on the quantities given in the manufacturer's instructions. Every dog has different requirements and—as in humans—where one dog will grow fat on

'DOES THIS COLLAR MAKE ME LOOK FAT?'

While humans may obsess about how they look and how trim their bodies are, many people believe that extra weight on their dogs is a good thing. The truth is, pets should not be over- or under-weight, as both can lead to or signal sickness. In order to tell how fit your pet is, run your hands over his ribs. Are his ribs buried under a layer of fat or are they sticking out considerably? If your pet is within his normal weight range, you should be able to feel the ribs easily. If you stand above him, the outline of his body should resemble an hourglass. Some breeds do tend to be leaner; while some are a bit stockier, but making sure your dog is the right weight for his breed will certainly contribute to his good health.

just a small portion, another will need double the quantity. So it is best to 'feed with your eyes.'

DIETS FOR SENIOR DOGS

As dogs get older, their metabolism changes. The older dog usually exercises less, moves more slowly and sleeps more. This change in lifestyle and physiological performance requires a change in diet. Since these changes take place slowly, they might not be recognisable; what is easily recognisable is weight gain. By continually feeding your dog an adult maintenance diet when it is slowing down metabolically, your dog will gain weight. Obesity in an older dog compounds the health problems that already accompany old age. Consider switching your Welsh to a food formulated especially for seniors around 8 years of age

DO DOGS HAVE TASTE BUDS?
Watching a dog 'wolf' or gobble his food, seemingly without chewing, leads an owner to wonder whether their dogs can taste anything. Yes, dogs have taste buds, with sensory perception of sweet, salty and sour. Puppies are born with fully mature taste buds.

or older, depending on the condition of the dog. So here as well, feed 'with your eyes.'

As your dog gets older, few of his organs function up to par. The kidneys slow down and the intestines become less efficient. These age-related factors are best handled with a change in diet and a change in feeding schedule to give smaller portions that are more easily digested. There is no single best diet for every older dog; it is up to you to find out which diet suits his need best.

When you see grey on the muzzle, you know your Welshie is getting older. This is the time to consult with your vet about possible dietary changes for your senior dog.

The pet Welshie's coat does not need much special care beyond regular brushing and combing; however, the ears have a tendency to dip into the dog's food and water bowls and the ends may need a bit of extra attention.

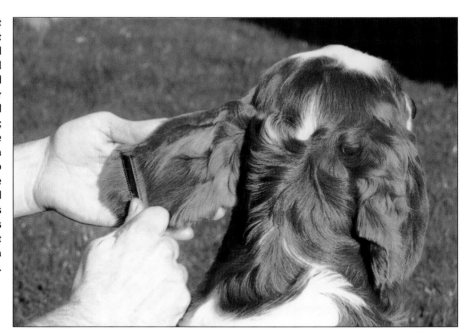

WATER

Just as your dog needs proper nutrition from his food, water is an essential 'nutrient' as well. Water keeps the dog's body properly hydrated and promotes normal function of the body's systems. During housebreaking it is necessary to keep an eye on how much water your Welsh Springer is drinking, but once he is reliably trained he should have access to clean fresh water at all times. Make sure that the dog's water bowl is clean, and change the water often.

You will find that your Welsh Springer Spaniel is a very sloppy drinker; he loves his water bowl and in his enthusiasm he will often not only put his mouth but also both front paws in the bowl. Or

CHANGE IN DIET

As your dog's caretaker, you know the importance of keeping his diet consistent, but sometimes when you run out of food or if you're on holiday, you have to make a change quickly. Some dogs will experience digestive problems but most will not. If you are planning on changing your dog's menu, do so gradually to ensure that your dog will not have any problems. Over a period of four to five days, slowly add some new food to your dog's old food, increasing the percentage of new food each day.

he will take one last mouthful of water and before swallowing it come to you to tell you how much he loves you! A special spaniel bowl may help you keep the kitchen floor clean.

EXERCISE

All dogs require some form of exercise, regardless of breed. A sedentary lifestyle is as harmful to a dog as it is to a person. The Welsh Springer Spaniel is a very lively and active breed that requires a lot of free exercise. He might like to come with you on a shopping expedition but what he needs is to run around free, preferably in exciting surroundings, like woods or fields, where he can develop his hunting instincts.

Owners often make mistakes in the exercise they give their dog. As the new puppy is an exciting thing, they often tend to give him too much exercise. It is only human to show off something you are very proud of, but it means that the small puppy is taken on too many walks. For a puppy up to six months the garden is big enough. Take him to the park once a day, to let him socialise and play with the other dogs for about 15 minutes. Once the puppy is about nine months old, you can extend the daily walks to an hour daily, and once he is a year old, his energy

DRINK, DRANK, DRUNK— MAKE IT A DOUBLE

In both humans and dogs, as well as most living organisms, water forms the major part of nearly every body tissue. Naturally, we take water for granted, but without it, life as we know it would cease.

For dogs, water is needed to keep their bodies functioning biochemically. Additionally, water is needed to replace the water lost while panting. Unlike humans who are able to sweat to dissipate heat, dogs must pant to cool down, thereby losing the vital water from their bodies needed to regulate their body temperatures. Humans lose electrolyte-containing products and other body-fluid components through sweating; dogs do not lose anything except water.

Water is essential always, but especially so when the weather is hot or humid or when your dog is exercising or working vigorously.

will be boundless.

We cannot stress the importance of exercise enough. It is essential to keep the dog's body fit, but it is also essential to his mental well-being. A bored dog will find something to do, which often manifests itself in some type of destructive behaviour. In this sense, it is essential for your mental well-being as well!

GROOMING

By grooming we mean the care for the dog's health, cleanliness, comfort and appearance, the way we keep him clean and tidy.

The coat of a Welsh Springer Spaniel is naturally straight, flat, soft to the touch, never wiry or wavy. It is sufficiently dense to be waterproof, thornproof and weatherproof. The back of the forelegs, the hindlegs above the hocks, chest and underside of the body are moderately feathered. The ears and tail are lightly feathered. The colour is a rich red and white, any pattern is acceptable and any white area may be flecked with red ticking.

You will find that this coat doesn't need much care as long as the dog is healthy and is brushed and combed regularly, at least once a week but preferably more often. Because of the silky texture of the coat, the hairs can easily form tangles and mats and a thorough combing session will prevent that. Don't worry when after a walk in bad weather your whiter than white Welsh comes home all muddy and dirty. After a bath and a good rub with a towel, you'll find he dries off in a warm room and the white is pearly white again. You will find that there really is no need to bath him often although owners often like to bath their bitch after she's had her season.

BRUSHING

Brushing should ideally be done every day. It takes little time but the daily attention is important for health reasons and, when you start with a puppy, for reasons of bonding with your dog and establishing control. Future show dogs need to become used to being examined and standing still and the daily brushing will help.

Daily brushing is effective for removing dead hair and stimulating the dog's natural oils to add shine and a healthy look to the coat. The combing is necessary to prevent tangles forming in such places as the armpits, behind the ears and in the feathers. At the same time you can check his ears, eyes and paws for possible cuts or thorns.

GROOMING EQUIPMENT

How much grooming equipment you purchase will depend on how much grooming you are going to do. Here are some basics:

- Natural bristle brush
- Slicker brush
- Metal comb
- Scissors
- Blaster
- Rubber mat
- Dog shampoo
- Spray hose attachment
- Ear cleaner
- Cotton wipes
- Towels
- Nail clippers

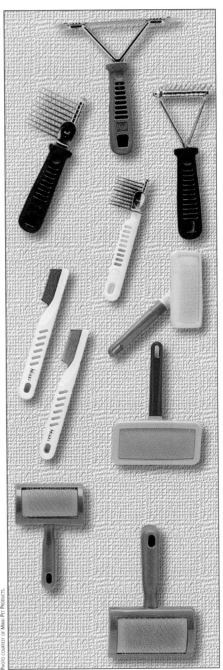

Your local pet shop will have a wide variety of grooming tools from which you can select what you'll need for your Welshie.

For brushing you can best use a natural, medium-hard bristle brush, a glove with a bristle brush or a slicker brush but be careful with that, you can easily hurt his skin. You need a comb for his ears and feathers and to remove dead hair.

TRIMMING

The coat needs trimming, though, but just once every three or four months. The coat on his body and head will stay flat and straight but his ears, throat, tail and feet will need trimming. You can always ask the breeder for help and it is greatly recommended and very rewarding if you learn to do this

PHOTO COURTESY OF MIKKI PET PRODUCTS.

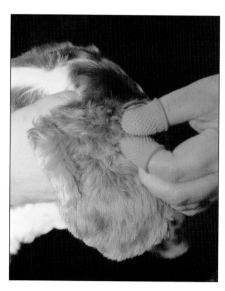

Excess hair on the ears can easily be removed with the finger-and-thumb method, using rubber 'thumblettes' to grip the hair.

yourself. Although he doesn't grow much coat the first seven or eight months of his life, the hair on his feet will grow rather quickly. If you remove this

The hair on the throat is trimmed with thinning shears.

superfluous hair, he will not only look tidier but also get used to having his feet trimmed at an early age.

Theoretically all trimming should be done with finger and thumb and a comb, which sometimes can be a laborious and time consuming process, but don't try to cut corners and use clippers or scissors because you will find that you have spoilt his silky and flat coat for ever.

Excess hair on the ears can be removed fairly easily from the ears by using the comb and finger-and thumb method (you can use a surgical glove to have a better grip) or a trimming knife, the one with teeth (not with a razor blade in it). The hair on the edges can be removed by using thinning scissors. If you hold the ear near the edge with one hand and cut with the other you can never cut in the dog's ear, which is very sensitive and can bleed profusely if cut. Use thinning scissors to cut the hair behind and below the ears, around the ear opening and on the inside of the earflap.

You will keep his ears troublefree by a regular cleaning of the outer section of the ear canal and if necessary use ear cleaner for the inner section.

The throat is trimmed as far down as the breastbone with

thinning scissors.

Untrimmed feet not only look untidy but can also be uncomfortable for the dog and bring a lot of dirt into the house. Trim the hair away between the pads on the underside of the feet—cut level with the pads. Trim the hair between the toes, pull up the hair between the toes and cut downwards and then cut round the feet.

The feathering on the hocks is trimmed with thinning scissors. Superfluous hair on the body should always be pulled out with finger and thumb.

Be prepared though: no matter how often you brush and trim your Welsh Springer, he will shed his hair and you will always find white hairs in the house. This is just one more reason to teach him right from the start not to sit on your chair or lie in your bed!

BATHING

Dogs do not need to be bathed as often as humans, but sometimes a bath will be necessary. It is therefore important that you accustom your pup to being bathed as a puppy, so that he is used to it when he grows up. You will have to bath your dog the day before a show and most owners like to bath their bitches after

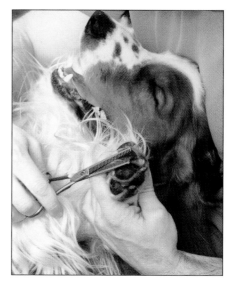

Trim the hair away between the footpads to keep the feet looking neat and to avoid irritation from excess hair.

they have been in season.

Before you are going to bath your dog check the coat for tangles. Make sure that your dog has a good non-slip surface

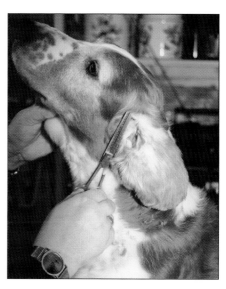

Thinning shears are also used on the inside of the ear.

SOAP IT UP

The use of human soap products like shampoo, bubble bath and hand soap can be damaging to a dog's coat and skin. Human products are too strong and remove the protective oils coating the dog's hair and skin (making him water-resistant). Use only shampoo made especially for dogs and you may like to use a medicated shampoo, which will always help to keep external parasites at bay.

to stand on. Begin by wetting the dog's coat. A shower or hose attachment is necessary for thoroughly wetting and rinsing the coat. Check the water temperature to make sure that it is neither too hot nor too cold. Fill his ear openings with cotton wool so that there is no chance of water or soap coming into the ear canals.

Next, apply shampoo to the dog's coat and work it into a good lather. You should purchase a shampoo that is made for dogs; do not use a product made for human hair. Wash the head last; you do not want shampoo to drip into the dog's eyes while you are washing the rest of his body. Work the shampoo all the way down to the skin. You can use this opportunity to check the

skin for any bumps, bites or other abnormalities. Do not neglect any area of the body – get all of the hard-to-reach places.

Once the dog has been thoroughly shampooed, he requires an equally thorough rinsing. Shampoo left in the coat can be irritating to the skin. Protect his eyes from the shampoo by shielding them with your hand and directing the flow of water in the opposite direction.

Be prepared for your dog to shake out his coat— you might want to stand back, but make sure you have a hold on the dog to keep him from running through the house.

BATHING BEAUTY

Once you are sure that the dog is thoroughly rinsed, squeeze the excess water out of the coat with your hand and dry him with a heavy towel. You may choose to use a blaster on his coat or just let it dry naturally. In cold weather, never allow your dog outside with a wet coat.

There are 'dry bath' products on the market, which are sprays and powders intended for spot cleaning, that can be used between regular baths, if necessary. They are not substitutes for regular baths, but they are easy to use for touch-ups as they do not require rinsing.

EAR CLEANING

The ears should be kept clean and any excess hair inside the ear should be trimmed. Ears can be cleaned with an ear cleaner made especially for dogs. Be on the lookout for any signs of infections or ear mite infestation and during the summer for grass-seeds that may be picked up from the grass by the ears and find their way into the ear canal. If your Welsh Springer Spaniel has been shaking his head or scratching at his ears frequently, this usually indicates a problem. Don't clean the ear canal yourself. If you poke into the ear canal with pincers and cotton wool you'll only succeed in aggravating things. Contact your vet before the condition gets serious.

If you check your spaniel's ears regularly and use the ear cleaner when the ear doesn't look 100% clean, you will find that the spaniel's reputation for ear-trouble is totally unfounded.

NAIL CLIPPING

Your Welsh should be accustomed to having his nails trimmed at an early age, since it will be part of your maintenance routine throughout his life. Not only does it look nicer, but also a dog with long nails can cause injury if he jumps up or if he scratches someone unintentionally. Also, a long nail has a better chance of ripping and bleeding, or causing feet to spread. A good rule of thumb is that if you can hear your dog's nails clicking on the floor when he walks, his nails are too long.

Before you start cutting make sure you can identify the 'quick' in each nail. The quick is a blood vessel that runs through the centre of each nail and grows rather close to the end. It will bleed profusely if accidentally cut, which will be quite painful for the dogs as it contains nerve endings. Keep

Ears can be kept clean with an ear cleaner made especially for dogs and a soft cotton wipe. Be careful not to probe into the ear.

Your pet shop will have special clippers for trimming your Welshie's nails. Shown here are the popular guillotine-style clippers.

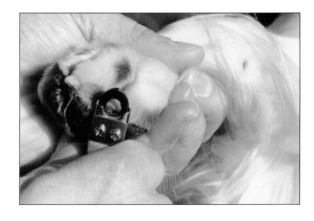

Clipping or grinding down your Welsh Springer Spaniel's nails is a must unless the dog spends a lot of time walking on hard surfaces.

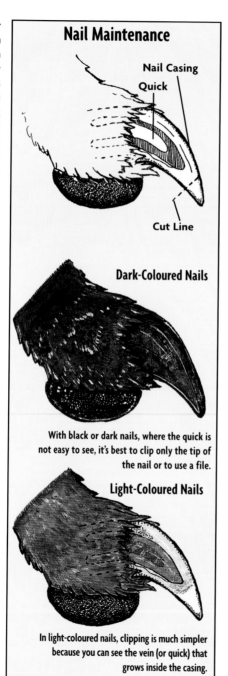

Nail Maintenance

Nail Casing

Quick

Cut Line

Dark-Coloured Nails

With black or dark nails, where the quick is not easy to see, it's best to clip only the tip of the nail or to use a file.

Light-Coloured Nails

In light-coloured nails, clipping is much simpler because you can see the vein (or quick) that grows inside the casing.

Clip only the bottom portion of the nail, avoiding the quick. If you cut into the quick, the nail will bleed and the dog will experiene pain. A styptic pencil will stop the bleeding. Reassure the injured dog by talking quietly to him.

some type of clotting agent on hand, such as a styptic pencil or styptic powder (the type used for shaving). This will stop the bleeding quickly when applied to the end of the cut nail. Do not panic if this happens, just stop the bleeding and talk soothingly to your dog. Once he has calmed down, move on to the next nail. It is better to clip a little at a time, particularly with black-nailed dogs.

Hold your pup steady as you begin trimming his nails; you do not want him to make any sudden movements or jump off the table. Talk to him soothingly and stroke his fur as

DEADLY DECAY

Did you know that periodontal disease (a condition of the bone and gums surrounding a tooth) can be fatal? Having your dog's teeth and mouth checked yearly can prevent it.

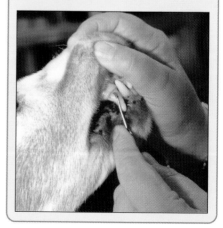

you clip. Holding his foot in your hand, simply take off the end of each nail in one quick clip. You can purchase nail clippers that are specially made for dogs; you may find the 'guillotine'-type the best ones to use.

If you feel all this is beyond you, you might prefer the use of a nail grinder. This is a small, battery operated contraption, that slowly grinds the nails. There is no fear of cutting into the quick and the dogs don't mind the slight buzzing sound of the grinder at all.

TRAVELLING WITH YOUR DOG

CAR TRAVEL

You should accustom your Welsh Springer Spaniel to riding in a car at an early age. If you are lucky the breeder has already taken the puppies in his car for a visit to the vet or just for a ride, so that when you come to take your puppy home

PEDICURE TIP
A dog that spends a lot of time outside on a hard surface, such as cement or pavement, will have his nails naturally worn down and may not need to have them trimmed as often, except maybe in the colder months when he is not outside as much. Regardless, it is best to get your dog accustomed to this procedure at an early age so that he is used to it. Some dogs are especially sensitive about having their feet touched, but if a dog has experienced it since he was young, he should not be bothered by it.

he knows what it is to be in a car. You will find that most spaniels love a ride in the car.

The best way for a dog to travel in a car is in his crate. You can use either the fibreglass or the wire crates. Another option is the specially made safety harness for dogs, which straps the dog in much like a seat belt. Do not let the dog

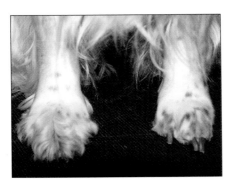

Before and after: (left) an untrimmed foot and (right) a trimmed foot with the nails cut.

LET THE SUN SHINE
Your dog needs daily sunshine for the same reason people do. Pets kept inside homes with curtains drawn against the sun suffer 'SAD' (Seasonal Affected Disorder) to the same degree as humans. We now know that sunlight must enter the iris and thus to the pineal gland to regulate the body's hormonal system and when we live and work in artificial light, both circadian rhythms and hormone balances are disturbed.

roam loose in the vehicle—this is very dangerous! If you should stop short, your dog can be thrown and injured. If the dog starts climbing on you and pestering you while you are driving, you will not be able to concentrate on the road. It is an unsafe situation for everyone—human and canine.

The best way to accustom your puppy to travelling in the car is by doing it gradually. Start with putting the puppy in the crate, while you sit behind the steering wheel. Talk to him and tell him how much he will enjoy this. Repeat this the next day and start the car; let the engine run for a couple of minutes. The next day you should drive around the block and slowly extend your trips. Drive to the park and let him have a quick run and feed him when you come home. Whatever you do, make it fun for him.

For long trips, be prepared to stop to let the dog relieve himself. Bring along whatever you need to clean up after him. You should also bring along some old towels and rags, should he have an accident in the car or despite your preparations become carsick.

AIR TRAVEL
As from March 1, 2000, the quarantine for animals travelling to Great Britain has been lifted and it will be possible to take a dog from the Continent into Great Britain. The dog must have had a rabies vaccination and a blood test has to performed six months after this vaccination to show that there is a sufficient anti-body titre in the blood. Also the dog has to be microchipped and to be treated for certain parasites and

ticks. For full information you can contact either the British Embassy in your own country or The Kennel Club in Great Britain.

The dog will be required to travel in a fibreglass crate and advance permission is always required. To help the dog be at ease, put one of his favourite toys in the crate with him. Do not feed the dog at least six hours before the trip to minimise his need to relieve himself. However, certain regulations specify that water must always be made available to the dog in the crate.

Make sure that your contact information is on his ID tags

TRAVEL TIP

When travelling, never let your dog off-lead in a strange area. Your dog could run away out of fear or decide to chase a passing squirrel or cat or simply want to stretch his legs without restriction—you might never see your canine friend again.

and on his crate. Animals travel in a different area of the plane than human passengers so every rule must be strictly adhered to so as to prevent the risk of getting separated from your dog. Should you plan to travel from the continent to Great Britain or vice versa for the first time, you

The back of this car has been partitioned off to give the dogs a safe area in which to ride and to keep them from disturbing the driver.

ON THE ROAD

If you are going on a long motor trip with your dog, be sure the hotels are dog friendly. Many hotels do not accept dogs. Also take along some ice that can be thawed and offered to your dog if he becomes overheated. Most dogs like to lick ice.

might consider taking the Shuttle where you go by train through the Channel Tunnel. This takes only 40 minutes and you stay in the car with the dog. You can also go by ferry; the Hoverspeed from Calais only takes 40 minutes. The authorities in Calais, Cherbourg, Caen, St. Malo and Le Havre, as well as in Portsmouth, Dover and Heathrow, have the facilities for checking your dog, his microchip and his papers. More ports should be able to do so in the near future.

BOARDING

So you want to take a family holiday—and you want to include all members of your family. You would probably make arrangements for accommodation ahead of time anyway, but this is especially important when travelling with a dog. You do not want to make an overnight stop at the only place around for miles to find out that they do not allow dogs. Also, you do not want to reserve a place for your family without mentioning that you are bringing a dog, because if it is against their policy you may not have a place to stay.

Alternatively, if you are travelling and choose not to bring your Welsh Springer Spaniel, you will have to make arrangements for him while you are away. Some options are to bring him to a neighbour's house to stay while you are away, to have a trusted neighbour pop in often or stay at your house, or bring your dog to a reputable boarding kennel. If you choose to board him at a kennel, you should stop by to see the facility and where the dogs are kept to make sure that it is clean. Talk to the owner or

VACCINATIONS

For international travel you will have to make arrangements well in advance (perhaps months), as countries' regulations pertaining to bringing in animals differ. There may be special health certificates and/or vaccinations that your dog will need before taking the trip; sometimes this has to be done within a certain time frame. In rabies-free countries, you will need to bring proof of the dog's rabies vaccination and there may be a quarantine period upon arrival.

the manager and see how he or she treats the dogs – do they spend time with the dogs, play with them, exercise them, etc.? You know that your Welsh will not be happy unless he gets regular activity. Also find out the kennel's policy on vaccinations and what they require. This is for all of the dogs' safety, since when dogs are kept together, there is a greater risk of diseases being passed from dog to dog.

IDENTIFICATION

Your Welsh is your valued companion and friend. That is why you always keep a close eye on him and you have made sure that he cannot escape from the garden or wriggle out of his collar and run away from you. However, accidents can happen and there may come a time when your dog unexpectedly gets separated from you. If this unfortunate event should occur,

the first thing on your mind will be finding him. Proper identification will increase the chances of his being returned to you safely and quickly. In many countries tattooing or micro-chipping the puppies before they leave the breeder is common practice and often done by the Kennel Club so that the number that is given to the puppy either as an earmark or via the microchip is a unique number that is also recorded on his pedigree.

An ear tattoo (enhanced for clarity).

Imagine if these dogs were not trained to HEEL?

Housebreaking and Training Your
WELSH SPRINGER SPANIEL

Living with an untrained dog is like owning a piano that you do not know how to play—it is a nice object to look at but it does not do much more than that to bring you pleasure. Now try taking piano lessons and suddenly the piano comes alive and brings forth magical sounds and rhythms that set your heart singing and your body swaying.

The same is true with your Springer. At first you enjoy seeing him around the house. He does not do much with you other than to need food, water and exercise. Come to think of it, he is a big responsibility and a lot of work. Often, he develops unacceptable behaviours that annoy and/or infuriate you to say nothing of bad habits that may end up costing you great sums of money. Not a good thing!

THE HAND THAT FEEDS
To a dog's way of thinking, your hands are like his mouth in terms of a defence mechanism. If you squeeze him too tightly, he might just bite you because that would be his normal response. This is not aggressive biting and, although all biting should be discouraged, you need the discipline in learning how to handle your dog.

Now enrol him in an obedience class. Teach him good manners as you learn how and why he behaves the way he does. Find out how to communicate with your dog and how to recognise and understand his communications with you. Suddenly the dog takes on a new role in your life—he is smart, interesting, well behaved and fun to be with, and he demonstrates his bond of devotion to you daily. In other words, your dog does wonders for your ego because he constantly reminds you that you are not only his leader, you are his hero! Miraculous things have happened—you have a wonderful dog (even your family and friends have noticed the transformation!) and you feel good about yourself.

Those involved with teaching dog obedience and counselling owners about their dogs' behaviour have discovered some interesting facts about dog ownership. For example, training dogs when they are puppies results in the highest rate of success in developing well-mannered and well-adjusted adult dogs. Training an older dog, say from six months to six years of age, can produce almost equal results providing that the owner accepts the dog's slower rate of learning capability and is willing to work patiently to help the dog succeed at developing to his fullest potential. Unfortunately, the patience factor is what many owners of untrained adult dogs lack, so they do not persist until their dogs are successful at learning particular behaviours.

Training a puppy, for example, aged 8 to 16 weeks (20 weeks at the most) is like working with a dry sponge in a pool of water. The pup soaks up whatever you show him and constantly looks for more things to do and learn. At this early age, his body is not yet producing hormones, and therein lies the reason for such a high rate of success. Without hormones, he is focused on his owners and not particularly interested in investigating other places, dogs, people, etc. You are his leader; his provider of food, water, shelter and security. Therefore, he latches onto you and wants to stay close. He will usually follow you from room to room, will not let you out of his sight when you are outdoors with him, and respond in like manner to the people and animals you encounter. If, for example, you greet a friend warmly, he will be happy to greet the person as well. If, however, you are hesitant, even anxious, about the approach of a stranger, he will respond accordingly.

REAP THE REWARDS

If you start with a normal, healthy dog and give him time, patience and some carefully executed lessons, you will reap the rewards of that training for the life of the dog. And what a life it will be! The two of you will find immeasurable pleasure in the companionship you have built together with love, respect and understanding.

Once the puppy begins to produce hormones, his natural curiosity emerges and he begins to investigate the world around him. It is at that time when you may notice that the untrained dog begins to wander away from you and even ignore your commands to stay close. When this behaviour becomes a problem, the owner has two choices: get rid of the dog or train him. It is strongly urged that you choose the latter option.

Occasionally there are no

Eventually your Welshie will have a favourite spot in which he will relieve himself.

classes available within a reasonable distance from the owner's home. Sometimes there are classes available but the tuition is too costly. Whatever the circumstances, the solution to the problem of lack of lesson availability lies within the pages of this book.

This chapter is devoted to helping you train your Welsh Springer Spaniel at home. If the recommended procedures are followed faithfully, you may expect positive results that will prove rewarding to both you and your dog.

Whether your Springer is a puppy or a mature adult, the methods of teaching and the techniques we use in training basic behaviours are the same. After all, no dog, whether puppy or adult, likes harsh or inhumane methods. All creatures, however, respond favourably to gentle motivational methods and sincere praise and encouragement. Now let us get started.

HOUSEBREAKING

You can train a puppy to relieve itself wherever you choose. For example, city dwellers often train their puppies to relieve themselves in the gutter because large plots of grass are not readily available. Suburbanites, on the other hand, usually have gardens to accommodate their dogs' needs.

Outdoor training includes such surfaces as grass, dirt and cement. Indoor training usually means training your dog to newspaper.

When deciding on the surface and location that you will want your puppy to use, be sure it is going to be permanent. Training your dog to grass and then changing your mind two months later is extremely difficult for both dog and owner.

Next, choose the command you will use each and every time you want your puppy to void. 'Hurry up' and 'Go make' are examples of commands commonly used by dog owners.

Get in the habit of asking the puppy, 'Do you want to go hurry up?' (or whatever your chosen relief command is) before you

THINK BEFORE YOU BARK
Dogs are sensitive to their master's moods and emotions. Use your voice wisely when communicating with your dog. Never raise your voice at your dog unless you are angry and trying to correct him. 'Barking' at your dog can become as meaningless as 'dogspeak' is to you. Think before you bark!

take him out. That way, when he becomes an adult, you will be able to determine if he wants to go out when you ask him. A confirmation will be signs of interest, wagging his tail, watching you intently, going to the door, etc.

Puppy needs to relieve himself after play periods, after each meal, after he has been sleeping and any time he indicates that he is looking for a place to urinate or defecate.

The urinary and intestinal tract muscles of very young puppies are not fully developed. Therefore, like human babies, puppies need to relieve themselves frequently.

Take your puppy out often— every hour for an eight-week-old, for example. The older the puppy, the less often he will need to relieve himself. Finally, as a mature healthy adult, he will require only three to five relief trips per day.

PARENTAL GUIDANCE
Training a dog is a life experience. Many parents admit that much of what they know about raising children they learned from caring for their dogs. Dogs respond to love, fairness and guidance, just as children do. Become a good dog owner and you may become an even better parent.

HOUSING

Since the types of housing and control you provide for your puppy have a direct relationship on the success of housetraining, we consider the various aspects of both before we begin training.

Bringing a new puppy home and turning him loose in your house can be compared to turning a child loose in a sports arena and telling the child that the place is all his! The sheer enormity of the place would be too much for him to handle.

Crate training has benefits for both dog and owner, but this isn't exactly what we mean by that!

Instead, offer the puppy clearly defined areas where he can play, sleep, eat and live. A room of the house where the family gathers is the most obvious choice. Puppies are social animals and need to feel a part of the pack right from the start. Hearing your voice, watching you while you are doing things and smelling you nearby are all

HONOUR AND OBEY

Dogs are the most honourable animals in existence. They consider another species (humans) as their own. They interface with you. You are their leader. Puppies perceive children to be on their level; their actions around small children are different from their behaviour around their adult masters.

positive reinforcers that he is now a member of your pack. Usually a sitting room, the kitchen or a nearby adjoining breakfast nook is ideal for providing safety and security for both puppy and owner.

Within that room there should be a smaller area which the puppy can call his own. A cubbyhole, a wire or fibreglass dog crate or a fenced (not boarded!) corner from which he can view the activities of his new family will be fine. The size of the area or crate is the key factor here. The area must be large enough for the puppy to lie down and stretch out as well as stand up

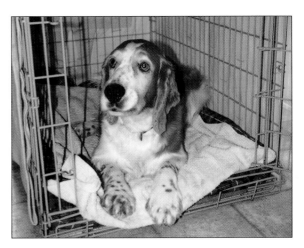

TRAINING TIP

Dogs will do anything for your attention. If you reward the dog when he is calm and resting, you will develop a well-mannered dog. If, on the other hand, you greet your dog excitedly and encourage him to wrestle with you, the dog will greet you the same way and you will have a hyperactive dog on your hands.

without rubbing his head on the top, yet small enough so that he cannot relieve himself at one end and sleep at the other without coming into contact with his droppings.

Dogs are, by nature, clean animals and will not remain close to their relief areas unless forced to do so. In those cases, they then become dirty dogs and usually remain that way for life.

The crate or cubby should be lined with a clean towel and offer one toy, no more. Do not put food or water in the crate, as eating and drinking will activate his digestive processes and ultimately defeat your purpose as well as make the puppy very uncomfortable as he attempts to 'hold it.'

CONTROL

By control, we mean helping the puppy to create a lifestyle pattern that will be compatible to that of

This Welshie seems to be right at home in his cosy crate. Once the dog is reliably trained, the crate door can be left open so the dog can come and go as he pleases.

TAKE THE LEAD

Do not carry your dog to his toilet area. Lead him there on a leash or, better yet, encourage him to follow you to the spot. If you start carrying him to his spot, you might end up doing this routine forever and your dog will have the satisfaction of having trained YOU.

PAPER CAPER

Never line your pup's sleeping area with newspaper. Puppy litters are usually raised on newspaper and, once in your home, the puppy will immediately associate newspaper with voiding. Never put newspaper on any floor while housetraining, as this will only confuse the puppy. If you are paper-training him, use paper in his designated relief area ONLY. Finally, restrict water intake after evening meals. Offer a few licks at a time—never let a young puppy gulp water after meals.

Start out by bringing your pup to the chosen relief area on lead. Once he is familiar with the routine, he will return to the spot on his own.

Never use newspapers to line the crate. Litters of pups are often raised on newspapers and therefore associate the papers with relieving themselves.

his human pack (YOU!). Just as we guide little children to learn our way of life, we must show the puppy when it is time to play, eat, sleep, exercise and even entertain himself.

Your puppy should always sleep in his crate. He should also learn that, during times of household confusion and excessive human activity such as at breakfast when family members are preparing for the day, he can play by himself in relative safety and comfort in his crate. Each time you leave the puppy alone, he should be crated. Puppies are chewers. They cannot tell the

ATTENTION!

Your dog is actually training you at the same time you are training him. Dogs do things to get attention. They usually repeat whatever succeeds in getting your attention.

difference between lamp cords, television wires, shoes, table legs, etc. Chewing into a television wire, for example, can be fatal to the puppy while a shorted wire can start a fire in the house.

If the puppy chews on the arm of the chair when he is alone, you will probably discipline him angrily when you get home. Thus, he makes the association that your coming home means he is going to be hit or punished. (He will not remember chewing the chair and is incapable of making the association of the discipline with his naughty deed.)

Other times of excitement, such as family parties, etc., can be fun for the puppy providing he

CANINE DEVELOPMENT SCHEDULE

It is important to understand how and at what age a puppy develops into adulthood. If you are a puppy owner, consult the following Canine Development Schedule to determine the stage of development your puppy is currently experiencing. This knowledge will help you as you work with the puppy in the weeks and months ahead.

Period	Age	Characteristics
First to Third	**Birth to Seven Weeks**	Puppy needs food, sleep and warmth, and responds to simple and gentle touching. Needs mother for security and disciplining. Needs littermates for learning and interacting with other dogs. Pup learns to function within a pack and learns pack order of dominance. Begin socialising with adults and children for short periods. Begins to become aware of its environment.
Fourth	**Eight to Twelve Weeks**	Brain is fully developed. Needs socialising with outside world. Remove from mother and littermates. Needs to change from canine pack to human pack. Human dominance necessary. Fear period occurs between 8 and 16 weeks. Avoid fright and pain.
Fifth	**Thirteen to Sixteen Weeks**	Training and formal obedience should begin. Less association with other dogs, more with people, places, situations. Period will pass easily if you remember this is pup's change-to-adolescence time. Be firm and fair. Flight instinct prominent. Permissiveness and over-disciplining can do permanent damage. Praise for good behaviour.
Juvenile	**Four to Eight Months**	Another fear period about 7 to 8 months of age. It passes quickly, but be cautious of fright and pain. Sexual maturity reached. Dominant traits established. Dog should understand sit, down, come and stay by now.

Note: These are approximate time frames. Allow for individual differences in puppies.

A wire crate is good for use inside the home. For puppies, however, never put the water bowl inside the crate, as this invites accidents when the puppy is crated.

can view the activities from the security of his crate. He is not underfoot and he is not being fed all sorts of titbits that will probably cause him stomach distress, yet he still feels a part of the fun.

SCHEDULE

As stated earlier, a puppy should be taken to his relief area each time he is released from his crate, after meals, after a play session,

On the table is not the proper place for your dog's food or water bowl. Bowls should be placed on the ground or on a specially made bowl stand, and the dog should eat his meals in the same spot each time.

when he first awakens in the morning (at age 8 weeks, this can mean 5 a.m.!) and whenever he indicates by circling or sniffing busily that he needs to urinate or defecate. For a puppy less than ten weeks of age, a routine of taking him out every hour is necessary. As the puppy grows, he will be able to wait for longer periods of time.

MEALTIME

Mealtime should be a peaceful time for your puppy. Do not put his food and water bowls in a high-traffic area in the house. For example, give him his own little corner of the kitchen where he can eat undisturbed and where he will not be underfoot. Do not allow small children or other family members to disturb the pup when he is eating.

Keep trips to his relief area short. Stay no more than five or six minutes and then return to the house. If he goes during that time, praise him lavishly and take him indoors immediately. If he does not, but he has an accident when you go back indoors, pick him up immediately, say 'No! No!' and return to his relief area. Wait a few minutes, then return to the house again. NEVER hit a puppy or rub his face in urine or excrement when he has an accident!

Once indoors, put the puppy in his crate until you have had

It cannot be stated enough that your garden must be 'puppy-proofed' and that there is nothing within the reach of your pup's curious nose and paws that could cause him harm.

time to clean up his accident. Then release him to the family area and watch him more closely than before. Chances are, his accident was a result of your not picking up his signal or waiting too long before offering him the opportunity to relieve himself. NEVER hold a grudge against the puppy for accidents.

Let the puppy learn that going outdoors means it is time to relieve himself, not play. Once trained, he will be able to play indoors and out and still differentiate between the times for play versus the times for relief.

Help him develop regular hours for naps, being alone, playing by himself and just resting, all in his crate. Encourage him to entertain himself while you are busy with your activities.

HOW MANY TIMES A DAY?

AGE	RELIEF TRIPS
To 14 weeks	10
14–22 weeks	8
22–32 weeks	6
Adulthood (dog stops growing)	4

These are estimates, of course, but they are a guide to the MINIMUM opportunities a dog should have each day to relieve itself.

THE CLEAN LIFE

By providing sleeping and resting quarters that fit the dog, and offering frequent opportunities to relieve himself outside his quarters, the puppy quickly learns that the outdoors (or the newspaper if you are training him to paper) is the place to go when he needs to urinate or defecate. It also reinforces his innate desire to keep his sleeping quarters clean. This, in turn, helps develop the muscle control that will eventually produce a dog with clean living habits.

Let him learn that having you near is comforting, but it is not your main purpose in life to provide him with undivided attention.

Each time you put a puppy in his crate tell him, 'Crate time!' (or whatever command you choose). Soon, he will run to his crate when he hears you say those words.

Always clean up after your dog, whether you're in a public place or your own garden.

In the beginning of his training, do not leave him in his crate for prolonged periods of time except during the night when everyone is sleeping. Make his experience with his crate a pleasant one and, as an adult, he will love his crate and willingly stay in it for a couple of hours.

Crate training provides safety for you, the puppy and the home. It also provides the puppy with a feeling of security, and that helps the puppy achieve self-confidence and clean habits.

Remember that one of the primary ingredients in housetraining your puppy is control. Regardless of your lifestyle, there will always be occasions when you will need to have a place where your dog can stay and be happy and safe. Crate training is the answer for now and in the future.

In conclusion, a few key elements are really all you need for a successful house and crate training method—consistency, frequency, praise, control and supervision. By following these procedures with a normal, healthy

THE SUCCESS METHOD

Success that comes by luck is usually short lived. Success that comes by well-thought-out proven methods is often more easily achieved and permanent. This is the Success Method. It is designed to give you, the puppy owner, a simple yet proven way to help your puppy develop clean living habits and a feeling of security in his new environment.

puppy, you and the puppy will soon be past the stage of 'accidents' and ready to move on to a full and rewarding life together.

ROLES OF DISCIPLINE, REWARD AND PUNISHMENT

Discipline, training one to act in accordance with rules, brings order to life. It is as simple as that. Without discipline, particularly in a group society, chaos reigns supreme and the group will eventually perish. Humans and

THE SUCCESS METHOD

1 Tell the puppy 'Crate time!' and place him in the crate with a small treat (a piece of cheese or half of a biscuit). Let him stay in the crate for five minutes while you are in the same room. Then release him and praise lavishly. Never release him when he is fussing. Wait until he is quiet before you let him out.

2 Repeat Step 1 several times a day.

3 The next day, place the puppy in the crate as before. Let him stay there for ten minutes. Do this several times.

4 Continue building time in five-minute increments until the puppy

stays in his crate for 30 minutes with you in the room. Always take him to his relief area after prolonged periods in his crate.

5 Now go back to Step 1 and let the puppy stay in his crate for five minutes, this time while you are out of the room.

6 Once again, build crate time in five-minute increments with you out of the room. When the puppy will stay willingly in his crate (he may even fall asleep!) for 30 minutes with you out of the room, he will be ready to stay in it for several hours at a time.

6 Steps to Successful Crate Training

This Welshie puppy knows the routine...he's gone out to do his business and now it's time to come back in!

canines are social animals and need some form of discipline in order to function effectively. They must procure food, protect their home base and their young and reproduce to keep the species going.

If there were no discipline in the lives of social animals, they would eventually die from starvation and/or predation by other stronger animals.

In the case of domestic canines, dogs need discipline in their lives in order to understand how their pack (you and other family members) function and how they must act in order to survive.

A large humane society in a highly populated area recently surveyed dog owners regarding their satisfaction with their relationships with their dogs. People who had trained their dogs were 75% more satisfied with their pets than those who had never trained their dogs.

Dr Edward Thorndike, a psychologist, established *Thorndike's Theory of Learning*, which states that a behaviour that results in a pleasant event tends to be repeated. A behaviour that results in an unpleasant event tends not to be repeated. It is this

PRACTICE MAKES PERFECT!

- Have training lessons with your dog every day in several short segments—three to five times a day for a few minutes at a time is ideal.
- Do not have long practice sessions. The dog will become easily bored.
- Never practise when you are tired, ill, worried or in an otherwise negative mood. This will transmit to the dog and may have an adverse effect on its performance.

Think fun, short and above all POSITIVE! End each session on a high note, rather than a failed exercise, and make sure to give a lot of praise. Enjoy the training and help your dog enjoy it, too.

KEEP SMILING

Never train your dog, puppy or adult, when you are angry or in a sour mood. Dogs are very sensitive to human feelings, especially anger, and if your dog senses that you are angry or upset, he will connect your anger with his training and learn to resent or fear his training sessions.

theory on which training methods are based today. For example, if you manipulate a dog to perform a specific behaviour and reward him for doing it, he is likely to do it again because he enjoyed the end result.

Occasionally, punishment, a penalty inflicted for an offence, is necessary. The best type of punishment often comes from an outside source. For example, a child is told not to touch the stove because he may get burned. He disobeys and touches the stove. In doing so, he receives a burn. From that time on, he respects the heat of the stove and avoids contact with it. Therefore, a behaviour that results in an unpleasant event tends not to be repeated.

A good example of a dog learning the hard way is the dog who chases the house cat. He is told many times to leave the cat alone, yet he persists in teasing the cat. Then, one day he begins chasing the cat but the cat turns and swipes a claw across the dog's face, leaving him with a painful gash on his nose. The final result is that the dog stops chasing the cat.

TRAINING EQUIPMENT

COLLAR AND LEAD

For a Welsh Springer Spaniel the collar and lead that you use for training must be sturdy, not too heavy for the dog, easy to work with and perfectly safe. A simple buckle collar is fine for most dogs. One who pulls mightily on the leash may require a chain choker collar.

TREATS

Have a bag of treats on hand. Something nutritious and easy to swallow works best; use a soft treat, a chunk of cheese or a piece of cooked chicken rather than a dry biscuit. By the time the dog

A puppy must be taught which behaviours are unacceptable. A Welshie (or any!) puppy sees no harm in a playful nip; it's up to you to teach him right from wrong.

PLAN TO PLAY

The puppy should also have regular play and exercise sessions when he is with you or a family member. Exercise for a very young puppy can consist of a short walk around the house or garden. Playing can include fetching games with a large ball or a special raggy. (All puppies teethe and need soft things upon which to chew.) Remember to restrict play periods to indoors within his living area (the family room, for example) until he is completely housetrained.

A pair of handsome young Welsh Springers with their collars and leads.

has finished chewing a dry treat, he will forget why he is being rewarded in the first place! Using food rewards will not teach a dog to beg at the table—the only way to teach a dog to beg at the table is to give him food from the table. In training, rewarding the dog with a

food treat away from the table will help him associate praise and the treats with learning new behaviours that obviously please his owner.

TRAINING BEGINS: ASK THE DOG A QUESTION

In order to teach your dog anything, you must first get his attention. After all, he cannot learn anything if he is looking away from you with his mind on something else.

To get his attention, ask him, 'School?' and immediately walk over to him and give him a treat as you tell him 'Good dog.' Wait a minute or two and repeat the routine, this time with a treat in your hand as you approach the dog to within a foot of him. Do not go directly to him, but stop about a foot short of him and hold out the treat as you ask, 'School?' He will see you approaching with a treat in your hand and most likely begin walking toward you. As you meet, give him the treat and praise again.

The third time, ask the question, have a treat in your hand and walk only a short distance toward the dog so that he must walk almost all the way to you. As he reaches you, give him the treat and praise again.

By this time, the dog will probably be getting the idea that if he pays attention to you, especially when you ask that question, it will pay off in treats and fun activities for him. In other words, he learns that 'school' means doing fun things with you that result in treats and positive attention for him.

Remember that the dog does not understand your verbal language, he only recognises sounds. Your question translates to a series of sounds for him, and those sounds become the signal to go to you and pay attention; if he does, he will get to interact with you plus receive treats and praise.

THE BASIC COMMANDS

TEACHING SIT

Now that you have the dog's attention, hold the lead in your left hand and the food treat in your right. Place your food hand at the dog's nose and let him lick the treat but not take it from you. Say 'Sit' and slowly raise your food hand from in front of the dog's nose up over his head so

> ### TRAINING RULES
> If you want to be successful in training your dog, you have four rules to obey yourself:
> 1. Develop an understanding of how a dog thinks.
> 2. Do not blame the dog for lack of communication.
> 3. Define your dog's personality and act accordingly.
> 4. Have patience and be consistent.

> ### 'NO' MEANS 'NO!'
> Dogs do not understand our language. They can be trained to react to a certain sound, at a certain volume. If you say 'No, Oliver' in a very soft pleasant voice it will not have the same meaning as 'No, Oliver!!' when you shout it as loud as you can. You should never use the dog's name during a reprimand, just the command NO!! Since dogs don't understand words, comics often use dogs trained with opposite meanings. Thus, when the comic commands his dog to SIT the dog will stand up, and vice versa.

that he is looking at the ceiling. As he bends his head upward, he will have to bend his knees to maintain his balance. As he bends his knees, he will assume a sit position. At that point, release the food treat and praise lavishly with comments such as 'Good dog! Good sit!', etc. Remember to always praise enthusiastically, because dogs relish verbal praise from their owners and feel so proud of themselves whenever they accomplish a behaviour.

Advanced exercises like agility training combine hand signals and voice commands to guide the dog through a series of obstacles.

You will not use food forever in getting the dog to obey your commands. Food is only used to teach new behaviours, and once the dog knows what you want when you give a specific command, you will wean him off the food treats but still maintain the verbal praise. After all, you will always have your voice with you, but there will be many times when you have no food rewards yet you expect the dog to obey.

OPEN MINDS

Dogs are as different from each other as people are. What works for one dog may not work for another. Have an open mind. If one method of training is unsuccessful, try another.

TEACHING DOWN

Teaching the down exercise is easy when you understand how the dog perceives the down position, and it is very difficult when you do not. In addition, teaching the down exercise using the wrong method can sometimes make the dog develop such a fear of the down that he either runs away when you say 'down' or he will simply refuse to do so.

Have the dog sit close alongside your left leg, facing in the same direction as you are. Hold the lead in your left hand and a food treat in your right. Now place your left hand lightly on the top of the dog's shoulders where they meet above the spinal cord. Do not push down on the dog's shoulders; simply rest your left hand there so you can guide the dog to lie down close to your left leg rather than to swing away from your side when he drops.

Now place the food hand at the dog's nose, say 'Down' very softly (almost a whisper), and slowly lower the food hand to the dog's front feet. When the food hand reaches the floor, begin moving it forward along the floor in front of the dog. Keep talking softly to the dog, saying things like, 'Do you want this treat? You can do this, good dog.' Your reassuring tone of voice will help calm the dog as he tries to follow the food hand in order to get the treat.

When the dog's elbows touch the floor, release the food and praise softly. Try to get the dog to maintain that down position for several seconds before you let him sit up again. The goal here is to get the dog to settle down and not feel threatened in the down position.

Teaching Stay

It is easy to teach the dog to stay in either a sit or a down position. Again, we use food and praise during the teaching process as we help the dog to understand exactly what it is that we are expecting him to do.

To teach the sit/stay, start with the dog sitting on your left side as before and hold the lead in your left hand. Have a food treat in your right hand and place your food hand at the dog's nose. Say 'Stay' and step out on your right foot to stand directly in front of the dog, toe to toe, as he licks and nibbles the treat. Be sure to keep his head facing upward to maintain the sit position. Count to

DOUBLE JEOPARDY
A dog in jeopardy never lies down. He stays alert on his feet because instinct tells him that he may have to run away or fight for his survival. Therefore, if a dog feels threatened or anxious, he will not lie down. Consequently, it is important to have the dog calm and relaxed as he learns the down exercise.

COMMAND STANCE
Stand up straight and authoritatively when giving your dog commands. Do not issue commands when lying on the floor or lying on your back on the sofa. If you are on your hands and knees when you give a command, your dog will think you are positioning yourself to play.

five and then swing around to stand next to the dog again with him on your left. As soon as you get back to the original position, release the food and praise lavishly.

To teach the down/stay, do the down as previously described. As soon as the dog lies down, say 'Stay' and step out on your right foot just as you did in the sit/stay. Count to five and then return to stand beside the dog with him on your left side. Release the treat and praise as always.

Within a week or ten days, you can begin to add a bit of distance between you and your dog when you leave him. When you do, use your left hand open with the palm facing the dog as a stay signal, much the same as the hand signal a police officer uses to stop traffic at an intersection. Hold the food treat in your right hand as before, but this time the food is not touching the dog's nose. He will watch the food hand and quickly learn that he is going to get that treat as soon as you return to his side.

When you can stand 1 metre away from your dog for 30 seconds, you can then begin building time and distance in both stays. Eventually, the dog can be expected to remain in the stay position for prolonged periods of time until you return to him or call him to you.

Always praise lavishly when he stays.

TEACHING COME

If you make teaching 'Come' a fun experience, you should never have a 'student' that does not love the game or that fails to come when called. The secret, it seems, is never to teach the word 'Come.'

At times when an owner most wants his dog to come when called, the owner is likely upset or anxious and he allows these feelings to come through in the tone of his voice when he calls his dog. Hearing that desperation in his owner's voice, the dog fears the results of going to him and therefore either disobeys outright

A properly trained Welsh Springer Spaniel should react energetically when he hears the command COME.

or runs in the opposite direction. The secret, therefore, is to teach the dog a game and, when you want him to come to you, simply play the game. It is practically a no-fail solution!

To begin, have several members of your family take a few food treats and each go into a different room in the house. Take turns calling the dog, and each person should celebrate the dog's finding him with a treat and lots of happy praise. When a person calls the dog, he is actually inviting the dog to find him and get a treat as a reward for 'winning.'

A few turns of the 'Where are you?' game and the dog will work out that everyone is playing the game and that each person has a big celebration awaiting his success at locating them. Once he learns to love the game, simply calling out 'Where are you?' will bring him running from wherever he is when he hears that all-important question.

The come command is recognised as one of the most important things to teach a dog, so it is interesting to note that there are trainers who work with thousands of dogs and never teach the actual word 'Come.' Yet these dogs will race to respond to a person who uses the dog's name followed by 'Where are you?' In one instance, for example, a woman has a 12-year-old

'COME' ... BACK

Never call your dog to come to you for a correction or scold him when he reaches you. That is the quickest way to turn a 'Come' command into 'Go away fast!' Dogs think only in the present tense, and your dog will connect the scolding with coming to you, not with the misbehaviour of a few moments earlier.

companion dog who went blind, but who never fails to locate her owner when asked, 'Where are you?'

Children, in particular, love to play this game with their dogs. Children can hide in smaller places like a shower stall or bath, behind a bed or under a table. The dog needs to work a little bit harder to find these hiding places, but when he does he loves to celebrate with a treat and a tussle with a favourite youngster.

TEACHING HEEL

Heeling means that the dog walks beside the owner without pulling. It takes time and patience on the owner's part to succeed at teaching the dog that he (the owner) will not proceed unless the dog is walking calmly beside him. Pulling out ahead on the lead is definitely not acceptable.

Begin with holding the lead in your left hand as the dog sits beside your left leg. Hold the loop

Your Welshie should walk politely on lead and keep up with your pace, as demonstrated by this Crufts 2000 Best of Breed winner as he makes his appearance in the Group ring.

end of the lead in your right hand but keep your left hand short on the lead so it keeps the dog in close next to you.

Say 'Heel' and step forward on your left foot. Keep the dog close to you and take three steps. Stop and have the dog sit next to you in what we now call the 'heel position.' Praise verbally, but do not touch the dog. Hesitate a moment and begin again with 'Heel,' taking three steps and stopping, at which point the dog is told to sit again.

Your goal here is to have the dog walk those three steps without pulling on the lead. When he will walk calmly beside you for three steps without pulling, increase the number of steps you take to five. When he will walk politely beside you while you take five steps, you can increase the length of your walk to ten steps. Keep increasing the length of your

stroll until the dog will walk quietly beside you without pulling as long as you want him to heel. When you stop heeling, indicate to the dog that the exercise is over by verbally praising as you pet him and say 'OK, good dog.' The 'OK' is used as a release word meaning that the exercise is finished and the dog is free to relax.

If you are dealing with a dog who insists on pulling you around, simply 'put on your brakes' and stand your ground until the dog realises that the two of you are not going anywhere until he is beside you and moving at your pace, not his. It may take some time just standing there to convince the dog that you are the leader and you will be the one to decide on the direction and speed of your travel.

Each time the dog looks up at you or slows down to give a slack lead between the two of you,

---

'WHERE ARE YOU?'

When calling the dog, do not say 'Come.' Say things like, 'Rover, where are you? See if you can find me! I have a biscuit for you!' Keep up a constant line of chatter with coaxing sounds and frequent questions such as, 'Where are you?' The dog will learn to follow the sound of your voice to locate you and receive his reward.

TRAINING TIP
If you are walking your dog and he suddenly stops and looks straight into your eyes, ignore him. Pull the leash and lead him into the direction you want to walk.

quietly praise him and say, 'Good heel. Good dog.' Eventually, the dog will begin to respond and within a few days he will be walking politely beside you without pulling on the lead. At first, the training sessions should be kept short and very positive; soon the dog will be able to walk nicely with you for increasingly longer distances. Remember also to give the dog free time and the opportunity to run and play when you have finished heel practice.

WEANING OFF FOOD IN TRAINING

Food is used in training new behaviours, yet once the dog understands what behaviour goes with a specific command, it is time to start weaning him off the food treats. At first, give a treat after each exercise. Then, start to give a treat only after every other exercise. Mix up the times when you offer a food reward and the times when you only offer praise so that the dog will never know when he is going to receive both food and praise and when he is going to receive only praise. This

is called a variable ratio reward system and it proves successful because there is always the chance that the owner will produce a treat, so the dog never stops trying for that reward. No matter what, ALWAYS give verbal praise.

OBEDIENCE CLASSES

As previously discussed, it is a good idea to enrol in an obedience class if one is available in your area. Many areas have dog clubs that offer basic obedience training as well as preparatory classes for obedience competition.

At obedience trials, dogs can earn titles at various levels of competition. The beginning levels of competition include basic behaviours such as sit, down, heel, etc. The more advanced levels of competition include more or less the same commands but more complex, such as staying while you disappear out of sight, heel without a lead etc.

The commands the dogs learn are extremely useful and the training classes are great fun for you and your dog.

HEELING WELL
Teach your dog to HEEL in an enclosed area. Once you think the dog will obey reliably and you want to attempt advanced obedience exercises such as off-lead heeling, test him in a fenced-in area so he cannot run away.

FAMILY TIES

If you have other pets in the home and/or interact often with the pets of friends and other family members, your pup will respond to those pets in much the same manner as you do. It is only when you show fear of or resentment toward another animal that he will act fearful or unfriendly.

country. For that he has to possess stamina and endurance, be merry and active and have a loyal, biddable and amiable temperament as he must work within a group of other dogs without quarrelling.

These are all qualities sought in a good worker: willingness to please the handler, readiness to go into cover, and willingness to learn. Some of these talents can be found in every Welsh, some of them are missing. Some Welshes are bad retrievers, gun-shy, will not take cover or are unstoppable. It is up to you to select the puppy that shows the most promise for work and that possesses at least as many qualifications as possible required for work. What you will find in nearly all of them is a lot of energy, a strong scenting power and intelligence.

Since there are a dozen times more English Springers and Cockers than Welsh Springers,

GUNDOG TRAINING

The spaniels' duties in the field consist of working close to the sportsman, to quest for game and to flush it and retrieve it when called upon to do so. The Springer is the dog for the rough shooter, i.e. the man who goes out by himself in search of game, be it fur or feather. The Welsh Springer Spaniel has often been referred to as 'the working man's spaniel.' He is not bred for glamour but purely and exclusively for work in rough

OBEDIENCE SCHOOL

A basic obedience beginner's class usually lasts for six to eight weeks. Dog and owner attend an hour-long lesson once a week and practise for a few minutes, several times a day, each day at home. If done properly, the whole procedure will result in a well-mannered dog and an owner who delights in living with a pet that is eager to please and enjoys doing things with his owner.

Retrieving practice is just one of the many aspects of gundog training.

TUG OF WALK?

If you begin teaching the heel by taking long walks and letting the dog pull you along, he misinterprets this action as an acceptable form of taking a walk. When you pull back on the lead to counteract his pulling, he reads that tug as a signal to pull even harder!

Welshes are often overlooked by sportsmen and not many compete in field trials, although professional trainers and judges confirm that they are good workers. Unfortunately, the pool of working stock is too small to create more dogs that can compete at field trials and can thus attract attention and gain popularity. On the other hand, whereas in Cockers and English Springers the breed has been divided into a 'working' and a 'show' type, each breeding according to their exclusive policies, in Welsh Springers we fortunately do not see such a split and the breed is very fortunate in having 'show' breeders that work their Welshes as well.

New owners should always be encouraged to start training their puppy. This is not only because the basic training is good for the puppy but also because it may enlarge the gene pool. Among these puppies there might be hidden talents and the more talent the better. Should your puppy be one of the talented ones and you persevere with the training, it will teach you both quite a lot. For you, as owner, training is

---

THE GOLDEN RULE

The golden rule of dog training is simple. For each 'question' (command), there is only one correct answer (reaction). One command = one reaction. Keep practising the command until the dog reacts correctly without hesitating. Be repetitive but not monotonous. Dogs get bored just as people do!

THE STUDENT'S STRESS TEST

During training sessions you must be able to recognise signs of stress in your dog such as:

- tucking his tail between his legs
- lowering his head
- shivering or trembling
- standing completely still or running away
- panting and/or salivating
- avoiding eye contact
- flattening his ears back
- urinating submissively
- rolling over and lifting a leg
- grinning or baring teeth
- aggression when restrained

If your four-legged student displays these signs he may just be nervous or intimidated. The training session may have been too lengthy with not enough praise and affirmation. Stop for the day and try again tomorrow.

This is a typical practice dummy used in the beginning stages of a gundog's retriever training.

interesting and useful and gives you a greater understanding of your dog. Moreover, for both of you, it is great fun. It will give purpose and pleasure to your daily walks and it will keep you both healthy and in good condition.

You have to start at an early age. Get as much information about training methods as possible and get practical help. If you have no practical knowledge of shooting and no experience of training, you need the advice and help of other people, which is probably best found in the breed club. If there are no training classes, you can teach your dog yourself from a good manual or you might try and find a professional trainer who can give you a couple of lessons. However, do remember that the lessons are to

CONSISTENCY PAYS OFF

Dogs need consistency in their feeding schedule, exercise and toilet breaks and in the verbal commands you use. If you use 'Stay' on Monday and 'Stay here, please' on Tuesday, you will confuse your dog. Don't demand perfect behaviour during training classes and then let him have the run of the house the rest of the day. Above all, lavish praise on your pet consistently every time he does something right. The more he feels he is pleasing you, the more willing he will be to learn.

FETCH!
Play fetch games with your puppy in an enclosed area where he can retrieve his toy and bring it back to you. Always use a toy or object designated just for this purpose. Never use a shoe, stocking or other item he may later confuse with those in your wardrobe or underneath your chair.

Julita Roxane completes the retrieve. She is shown here at a 1994 field trial in which she had the best performance of the day.

teach the handlers and the handler has to teach his dog. Nobody can do that for you and you must be prepared to put a lot of time and effort into the instruc-tion. Rest assured that the results are well worth it!

The basis for every training is obedience and that is where you start with your puppy when it is

A properly trained Welsh Springer Spaniel will locate a downed bird and bring it back with a soft mouth, meaning that he will not bite into and/or damage the bird. This is Julita Ruella participating in a field trial.

FEAR AGGRESSION

Pups who are subjected to physical abuse during training commonly end up with behavioural problems as adults. One common result of abuse is fear aggression, in which a dog will lash out, bare his teeth, snarl and finally bite someone by whom he feels threatened. For example, your daughter may be playing with the dog one afternoon. As they play hide-and-seek, she backs the dog into a corner, and as she attempts to tease him playfully, he bites her hand. Examine the cause of this behaviour. Did your daughter ever hit the dog? Did someone who resembles your daughter hit or scream at the dog? Fortunately, fear aggression is relatively easy to correct. Have your daughter engage in only positive activities with the dog, such as feeding, petting and walking. She should not give any corrections or negative feedback. If the dog still growls or cowers away from her, allow someone else to accompany them. After approximately one week, the dog should feel that he can rely on her for many positive things, and he will also be prevented from reacting fearfully towards anyone who might resemble her.

listen to his name and then to sit on command. These are simple exercises and can be done in the house or in the garden.

Then you introduce him to retrieving. Use a small object such as a rolled up sock or glove, rabbit skin or a wing of a bird. If you throw the object a few yards ahead of your puppy, he will run to it and pick it up. Call him by his name and encourage him to bring it back to you. Don't be discouraged if your puppy thinks this is a lovely game and runs off with the object! If he does that, move away from him, calling him by his name. If he runs off again the second time, have him on a

SAFETY FIRST

While it may seem that the most important things to your dog are eating, sleeping and chewing the upholstery on your furniture, his first concern is actually safety. The domesticated dogs we keep as companions have the same pack instinct as their ancestors who ran free thousands of years ago. Because of this pack instinct, your dog wants to know that he and his pack are not in danger of being harmed, and that his pack has a strong, capable leader. You must establish yourself as the leader early on in your relationship. That way your dog will trust that you will take care of him and the pack, and he will accept your commands without question.

about three months old. By starting with the elementary exercises you get to know your puppy and gain his confidence and affection. First teach him to

'Found it!'
Julita Regal
Request
practices with
a different
type of
dummy; this
one resembles
a bird.

light line, so that you can—very lightly—pull him in while calling his name. But always remember to reward him whenever possible. Don't make the lessons too long, from 5 to 20 minutes a day is more than enough to keep it fun for your puppy and for you.

As most of the time is spent on correcting mistakes, it is important that you try and think ahead and anticipate what the puppy will do next, so that you avoid mistakes. Once he has acquired a bad habit you will have to start all over again.

After a couple of months you can teach him to heel and to sit

and stay on command. Make the distance between you and him greater every day and do it slowly. You achieve more when the puppy makes slow but steady progress than by going too fast

KEEP SMILING
Never train your dog, puppy or adult, when you are angry or in a sour mood. Dogs are very sensitive to human feelings, especially anger, and if your dog senses that you are angry or upset, he will connect your anger with his training and learn to resent or fear his training sessions.

French Trialer Welsh Fargo's Cherokee Indian Squaw.

quite painful and forcing him to pick it up would do irreparable harm to his willingness to retrieve.

Right from the start you should have prepared your puppy to accept loud bangs; in fact, this is something the breeder should have done when the puppies were just a couple of weeks old. Start with clapping your hands, banging the feed bowls or a bucket etc. If he shows no fear of such noises, you can introduce him to a starting pistol. Have somebody hold the pup and make it sit. You stand away from him while you fire. If he is steady, do not forget to praise him. If that goes well, shorten the distance. He can be introduced to the shotgun later but he has to get used to the shot first and learn to sit to heel with you firing over his head first.

You can also use a dummy launcher which will teach him to sit to shot, to mark and to retrieve.

Do not forget to introduce him to water. Start in the summer and find a still pond with shelving sides for his first lessons. He will love the water and learn to plunge in boldly to retrieve.

By the time your puppy is eight or nine months old, knows his basic obedience and has learnt to retrieve and use his nose, you can join a training

and risking constant repetition of the exercise. Remember also to end each lesson with a mastered exercise and praise. Never end with failure.

The next lesson is to encourage him to use his nose. By dragging a piece of tripe you can make a trail for him to work out. You can also throw an object into light cover, out of sight and encourage your Welsh to locate and then to retrieve it. You must be very careful with the puppy when he is teething because picking up the object might be class. Depending on his natural aptitude you can train for spaniel trials, field and working trials, working tests, tracking and more.

SNIFFER DOG TRAINING

A new 'career' has been discovered for spaniels as sniffer dogs. Sniffer dogs are used to find drugs, explosives and recently also cigarettes, hidden in cars, luggage and freight.

Several hundred dogs are being trained each year and for a greater part the training runs on parallel lines with the gundog training, i.e. as far as the dogs discovering the quarry. The dogs are being trained with dummies which contain a quantity of the target substance.

It seems that the Spaniels have taken over this job from the Retrievers, Spaniels having better scenting powers and being able to work fully concentrated for longer periods.

OTHER ACTIVITIES FOR LIFE

Whether a dog is trained in the structured environment of a class or alone with his owner at home, there are many activities that can bring fun and rewards to both owner and dog once they have mastered basic control.

Teaching the dog to help out around the home, in the garden or on the farm provides great satisfaction to both dog and owner. In addition, the dog's help

makes life a little easier for his owner and raises his stature as a valued companion to his family. It helps give the dog a purpose; it helps to keep his mind occupied and provides an outlet for his energy.

Backpacking is an exciting and healthy activity that the dog can be taught without assistance from more than his owner. The exercise of walking and climbing is good for man and dog alike, and the bond that they develop together is priceless.

Julita Rain Speckle retrieving the rabbit during a field test in 1995.

HELPING PAWS

Your dog may not be the next Lassie, but every pet has the potential to do some tricks well. Identify his natural talents and hone them. Is your dog always happy and upbeat? Teach him to wag his tail or give you his paw on command. Real homebodies can be trained to do household chores, such as carrying dirty washing or retrieving the morning paper.

If you are interested in participating in organised competition with your Springer there are other activities apart from obedience in which you and your dog can become involved. Agility is a popular and enjoyable sport where dogs run through an obstacle course that includes various jumps, tunnels and other exercises to test the dog's speed and co-ordination. The owners often run through the course beside their dogs to give commands and to guide them through the course. Although competitive, the focus is on fun— it's fun to do and fun to watch, as well as great exercise.

ON YOUR OWN

Occasionally, a dog and owner who have not attended formal classes have been able to earn entry-level titles by obtaining competition rules and regulations from a local kennel club and practising on their own to a degree of perfection. Obtaining the higher level titles, however, almost always requires extensive training under the tutelage of experienced instructors. In addition, the more difficult levels require more specialised equipment whereas the lower levels do not.

Julita Rain Speckle completing a water retrieve.

Health Care of Your
WELSH SPRINGER SPANIEL

Dogs suffer many of the same physical illnesses as people. They might even share many of the same psychological problems. Since people usually know more about human diseases than canine maladies, many of the terms used in this chapter will be familiar but not necessarily those used by veterinary surgeons. We will use the term *x-ray*, instead of the more acceptable term *radiograph*. We will also use the familiar term *symptoms* even though dogs don't have symptoms, which are verbal descriptions of the patient's feelings; dogs have *clinical signs*. Since dogs can't speak, we have to look for clinical signs...but we still use the term symptoms in this book.

As a general rule, medicine is practised. That term is not arbitrary. Medicine is a constantly changing art as we learn more and more about genetics, electronic aids (like CAT scans) and daily laboratory advances. There are many dog maladies, like canine hip dysplasia, which are not universally treated in the same manner. Some veterinary surgeons opt for surgery more often than others do.

Before you buy a dog, meet and interview the veterinary surgeons in your area. Take everything into consideration; discuss background, specialities, fees, emergency policies, etc.

SELECTING A VETERINARY SURGEON

Your selection of a veterinary surgeon should not be based upon personality (as most are) but upon their convenience to your home. You want a vet who is close because you might have emergencies or need to make multiple visits for treatments. You want a vet who has services that you might require such as tattooing and grooming, as well as sophisticated pet supplies and a good reputation for ability and responsiveness. There is nothing more frustrating than having to wait a day or more to get a response from your veterinary surgeon.

All veterinary surgeons are licensed and their diplomas

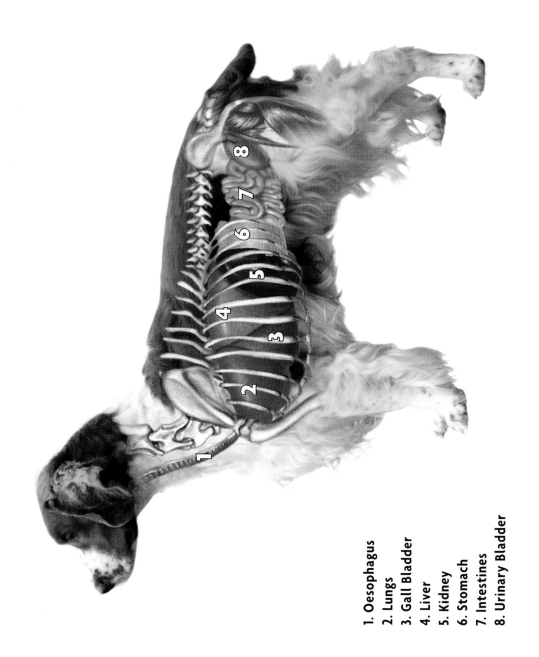

1. Oesophagus
2. Lungs
3. Gall Bladder
4. Liver
5. Kidney
6. Stomach
7. Intestines
8. Urinary Bladder

Internal Organs of the Welsh Springer Spaniel

and/or certificates should be displayed in their waiting rooms. There are, however, many veterinary specialities that usually require further studies and internships. There are specialists in heart problems (veterinary cardiologists), skin problems (veterinary dermatologists), teeth and gum problems (veterinary dentists), eye problems (veterinary ophthalmologists) and x-rays (veterinary radiologists), as well as vets who have specialities in bones, muscles or other organs. Most veterinary surgeons do routine surgery such as neutering, stitching up wounds and docking tails for those breeds in which such is required for show purposes. When the problem affecting your dog is serious, it is not unusual or impudent to get another medical opinion, although in Britain you are obliged to advise the vets concerned about this. You might also want to compare costs among several veterinary surgeons. Sophisticated health care and veterinary services can be very costly. Important decisions are often based upon financial considerations.

PREVENTATIVE MEDICINE
It is much easier, less costly and more effective to practise preventative medicine than to fight bouts of illness and disease. Properly bred puppies come from parents

Breakdown of Veterinary Income by Category

%	Category
2%	Dentistry
4%	Radiology
12%	Surgery
15%	Vaccinations
19%	Laboratory
23%	Examinations
25%	Medicines

A typical American vet's income, categorised according to services provided. This survey dealt with small-animal practices.

who were selected based upon their genetic disease profile. Their mothers should have been vaccinated, free of all internal and external parasites and properly nourished. For these reasons, a visit to the veterinary surgeon who cared for the dam is recommended. The dam can pass on disease resistance to her puppies, which can last for eight to ten weeks. She can also pass on parasites and many infections. That's why you should visit the veterinary surgeon who cared for the dam.

VACCINATION SCHEDULING
Most vaccinations are given by injection and should only be done by a veterinary surgeon. Both he and you should keep a record of the date of the injection, the identification of the vaccine and the amount given. Some vets give a first vaccination at eight weeks, but most dog breeders prefer the

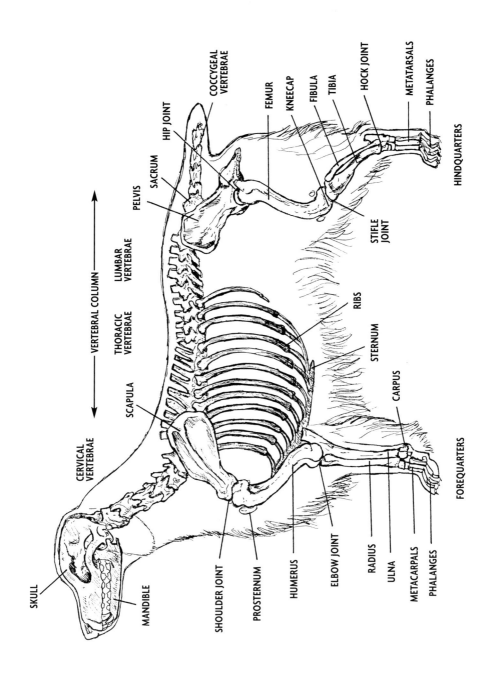

COCCYGEAL VERTEBRAE

HIP JOINT

FEMUR

KNEECAP

FIBULA

TIBIA

HOCK JOINT

METATARSALS

PHALANGES

SACRUM

PELVIS

HINDQUARTERS

STIFLE JOINT

LUMBAR VERTEBRAE

VERTEBRAL COLUMN

THORACIC VERTEBRAE

RIBS

SCAPULA

STERNUM

CARPUS

CERVICAL VERTEBRAE

FOREQUARTERS

SKULL

MANDIBLE

SHOULDER JOINT

PROSTERNUM

HUMERUS

ELBOW JOINT

RADIUS

ULNA

METACARPALS

PHALANGES

Skeletal Structure of the Welsh Springer Spaniel

course not to commence until about ten weeks because of negating any antibodies passed on by the dam. The vaccination scheduling is usually based on a 15-day cycle. You must take your vet's advice regarding when to vaccinate as this may differ according to the vaccine used. Most vaccinations immunize your puppy against viruses.

The usual vaccines contain immunizing doses of several different viruses such as distemper, parvovirus, parain-fluenza and hepatitis although some veterinary surgeons recommend separate vaccines for each disease. There are other vaccines available when the puppy is at risk. You should rely upon professional advice. This is especially true for the booster-shot programme. Most vaccination programmes require a booster when the puppy is a year old and once a year thereafter. In some cases, circumstances may require more or less frequent immuniza-tions. Kennel cough, more formally known as tracheobron-chitis, is treated with a vaccine that is sprayed into the dog's nostrils. Kennel cough is usually included in routine vaccination, but this is often not so effective as for other major diseases.

WEANING TO FIVE MONTHS OLD
Puppies should be weaned by the time they are about two months old. A puppy that remains for at least eight weeks with its mother and littermates usually adapts better to other dogs and people later in its life.

Some new owners have their puppy examined by a veterinary surgeon immediately, which is a good idea. Vaccination programmes usually begin when the puppy is very young.

The puppy will have its teeth examined and have its skeletal conformation and general health checked prior to certification by the veterinary surgeon. Puppies in certain breeds have problems with their kneecaps, cataracts and other eye problems, heart murmurs and undescended testicles. They may also have personality problems and your veterinary surgeon might have training in temperament evaluation.

FIVE TO TWELVE MONTHS OF AGE
Unless you intend to breed or show your dog, neutering the puppy at six months of age is recommended. Discuss this with your veterinary surgeon. Neutering has proven to be extremely beneficial to both male and female puppies. Besides eliminating the possibility of pregnancy, it inhibits (but does not prevent) breast cancer in bitches and prostate cancer in male dogs. Under no circumstances should a bitch be spayed prior to her

HEALTH AND VACCINATION SCHEDULE

Age in Weeks:	6TH	8TH	10TH	12TH	14TH	16TH	20-24TH	1 YR
Worm Control	✔	✔	✔	✔	✔	✔	✔	
Neutering								✔
Heartworm*		✔		✔		✔	✔	
Parvovirus	✔		✔		✔		✔	✔
Distemper		✔		✔		✔		✔
Hepatitis		✔		✔		✔		✔
Leptospirosis								✔
Parainfluenza	✔		✔		✔			✔
Dental Examination		✔					✔	✔
Complete Physical		✔					✔	✔
Coronavirus				✔			✔	✔
Kennel Cough	✔							
Hip Dysplasia								✔
Rabies*							✔	

Vaccinations are not instantly effective. It takes about two weeks for the dog's immunization system to develop antibodies. Most vaccinations require annual booster shots. Your veterinary surgeon should guide you in this regard.
*Not applicable in the United Kingdom

first season.

Your veterinary surgeon should provide your puppy with a thorough dental evaluation at six months of age, ascertaining whether all the permanent teeth have erupted properly. A home dental care regimen should be initiated at six months, including brushing weekly and providing good dental devices (such as nylon bones). Regular dental care promotes healthy teeth, fresh breath and a longer life.

ONE TO SEVEN YEARS

Once a year, your grown dog should visit the vet for an examination and vaccination boosters, if needed. Some vets recommend blood tests, thyroid level check and dental evaluation to accompany these annual visits. A thorough clinical evaluation by the vet can provide critical background information for your dog. Blood tests are often performed at one year of age, and dental examinations around the third or fourth birthday. In the long run, quality preventative care for your pet can save money, teeth and lives.

SKIN PROBLEMS IN WELSH SPRINGERS

Veterinary surgeons are consulted by dog owners for skin problems more than any other group of diseases or maladies. Dogs' skin is almost as sensitive as human skin and both suffer almost the same ailments (though the occurrence of acne in dogs is rare!). For this reason, veterinary dermatology has developed into a speciality practised by many veterinary surgeons.

Since many skin problems have visual symptoms that are almost identical, it requires the skill of an experienced veterinary dermatologist to identify and cure many of the more severe skin disorders. Pet shops sell many treatments for skin problems but most of the treatments are directed at symptoms and not the underlying problem(s). If your dog is suffering from a skin disorder, you should seek professional assistance as quickly as possible. As with all diseases, the earlier a problem is identified and treated, the more successful is the cure.

HEREDITARY SKIN DISORDERS

Veterinary dermatologists are currently researching a number of skin disorders that are believed to have a hereditary basis. These inherited diseases are transmitted by both parents, who appear (phenotypically) normal but have a recessive gene for the disease, meaning that they carry, but are not affected by, the disease. These diseases pose serious problems to breeders because in some instances there is no method of identifying carriers. Often the secondary diseases associated with these skin conditions are even more debilitating than the disorder itself, including cancers and respiratory problems; others can be lethal.

Among the hereditary skin disorders, for which the mode of inheritance is known, are: acrodermatitis, cutaneous asthenia (Ehlers-Danlos syndrome), sebaceous adenitis, cyclic hematopoiesis, dermatomyositis, IgA deficiency, colour dilution alopecia and nodular dermatofibrosis. Some of these disorders are limited to one or two breeds and others affect a large number of breeds. All inherited diseases must be diagnosed and treated by a veterinary specialist.

PARASITE BITES

Many of us are allergic to insect bites. The bites itch, erupt and may even become infected. Dogs have the same reaction to fleas, ticks and/or mites. When an insect lands on you, you have the chance to whisk it away with your hand. Unfortunately, when your dog is bitten by a flea, tick or mite, it can only scratch it away or bite it. By the time the dog has been bitten, the parasite has done some of its damage. It may also have laid eggs to cause further problems in the near future. The itching from parasite bites is probably due to the saliva injected into the site when the parasite sucks the dog's blood.

AUTO-IMMUNE SKIN CONDITIONS

Auto-immune skin conditions are commonly referred to as being allergic to yourself, while allergies are usually inflammatory reactions to an outside stimulus. Auto-immune diseases cause serious damage to the tissues that are involved.

The best known auto-immune disease is lupus, which affects people as well as dogs. The symptoms are variable and may affect the kidneys, bones, blood chemistry and skin. It can be fatal to both dogs and humans, though it is not thought to be transmissible. It is usually successfully treated with cortisone, prednisone or a similar corticosteroid, but extensive use of these drugs can have harmful side effects.

ACRAL LICK GRANULOMA

Many large dogs have a very poorly understood syndrome called acral lick granuloma. The manifestation of the problem is the dog's tireless attack at a specific area of the body, almost always the legs or paws. They lick so intensively that they remove the hair and skin, leaving an ugly, large wound.

AIRBORNE ALLERGIES

Another interesting allergy is pollen allergy. Humans have hay fever, rose fever and other fevers with which they suffer during the pollinating season. Many dogs suffer the same allergies. When the pollen count is high, your dog might suffer but don't expect him to sneeze and have a runny nose like humans. Dogs react to pollen allergies the same way they react to fleas—they scratch and bite.

Dogs, like humans, can be tested for allergens. Discuss the testing with your veterinary dermatologist.

FOOD PROBLEMS

FOOD ALLERGIES

Dogs are allergic to many foods that are best-sellers and highly recommended by breeders and veterinary surgeons. Changing the brand of food that you buy may not eliminate the problem if the element to which the dog is allergic is contained in the new brand.

Recognising a food allergy is difficult. Humans vomit or have rashes when they eat a food to which they are allergic. Dogs neither vomit nor (usually) develop a rash. They react in the same manner as they do to an airborne or flea allergy; they itch, scratch and bite, thus making the diagnosis extremely difficult. While pollen allergies and parasite bites are usually seasonal, food allergies are year-round problems.

FOOD INTOLERANCE

Food intolerance is the inability of the dog to completely digest certain foods. Puppies that may have done very well on their mother's milk may not do well on cow's milk. The rest of this food intolerance may be loose bowels, passing gas and stomach pains. These are the only obvious symptoms of food intolerance and that makes diagnosis difficult.

TREATING FOOD PROBLEMS

It is possible to handle food allergies and food intolerance yourself. Put your dog on a diet that it has never had. Obviously if it has never eaten this new food it can't have been allergic or intolerant of it. Start with a single ingredient that is not in the dog's diet at the present time. Ingredients like chopped beef or fish are common in dogs' diets, so try something more exotic like rabbit, pheasant or even just vegetables. Keep the dog on this diet (with no additives) for a month. If the symptoms of food allergy or

> ## BE CAREFUL WHERE YOU WALK YOUR DOG
> Dogs who have been exposed to lawns sprayed with herbicides have double and triple the rate of malignant lymphoma. Town dogs are especially at risk, as they are exposed to tailored lawns and gardens. Dogs perspire and absorb through their footpads. Be careful where your dog walks and always avoid any area that appears yellowed from chemical overspray.

intolerance disappear, chances are your dog has a food allergy.

Don't think that the single ingredient cured the problem. You still must find a suitable diet and ascertain which ingredient in the old diet was objectionable. This is most easily done by adding ingredients to the new diet one at a time. Let the dog stay on the modified diet for a month before you add another ingredient. Eventually, you will determine the ingredient that caused the adverse reaction.

An alternative method is to carefully study the ingredients in the diet to which your dog is allergic or intolerant. Identify the main ingredient in this diet and eliminate the main ingredient by buying a different food that does not have that ingredient. Keep experimenting until the symptoms disappear.

EXTERNAL PARASITES

Of all the problems to which dogs are prone, none is more well known and frustrating than fleas. Flea infestation is relatively simple to cure but difficult to prevent. Parasites that are harboured inside the body are a bit more difficult to eradicate but they are easier to control.

FLEAS

To control a flea infestation you have to understand the flea's life cycle. Fleas are often thought of as a summertime problem but centrally heated homes have changed the patterns and fleas can be found at any time of the year. The most effective method of flea control is a two-stage approach: one stage to kill the adult fleas, and the other to control the development of pre-adult fleas. Unfortunately, no single active ingredient is effective against all stages of the life cycle.

LIFE CYCLE STAGES

During its life, a flea will pass through four life stages: egg, larva, pupa and adult. The adult stage is the most visible and irritating stage of the flea life cycle and this is why the majority of flea-control products concentrate on this stage.

A scanning electron micrograph (S. E. M.) of a dog flea, *Ctenocephalides canis.*

Magnified head of a dog flea, *Ctenocephalides canis.*

A Look at Fleas

Fleas have been around for millions of years and have adapted to changing host animals. They are able to go through a complete life cycle in less than one month or they can extend their lives to almost two years by remaining as pupae or cocoons. They do not need blood or any other food for up to 20 months.

They have been measured as being able to jump 300,000 times and can jump 150 times their length in any direction including straight up. Those are just a few of the reasons why they are so successful in infesting a dog!

The fact is that adult fleas account for only 1% of the total flea population, and the other 99% exist in pre-adult stages, i.e. eggs, larvae and pupae. The pre-adult stages are barely visible to the naked eye.

THE LIFE CYCLE OF THE FLEA

Eggs are laid on the dog, usually in quantities of about 20 or 30, several times a day. The female adult flea must have a blood meal before each egg-laying session. When first laid, the eggs will cling to the dog's fur, as the eggs are still moist. However, they will quickly dry out and fall from the dog, especially if the dog moves around or scratches. Many eggs will fall off in the dog's favourite area or an area in which he spends a lot of time, such as his bed.

Once the eggs fall from the dog onto the carpet or furniture, they will hatch into larvae. This takes from one to ten days. Larvae are not particularly mobile, and will usually travel only a few inches from where they hatch. However, they do have a tendency to move away from light and heavy traffic—under furniture and behind doors are common places to find high quantities of flea larvae.

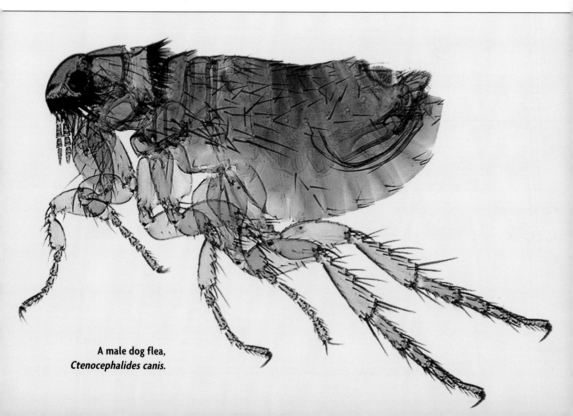

A male dog flea,
Ctenocephalides canis.

The flea larvae feed on dead organic matter, including adult flea faeces, until they are ready to change into adult fleas. Fleas will usually remain as larvae for around seven days. After this period, the larvae will pupate into protective pupae. While inside the pupae, the larvae will undergo metamorphosis and change into adult fleas. This can take as little time as a few days, but the adult fleas can remain inside the pupae waiting to hatch for up to two years. The pupae are signalled to hatch by certain stimuli, such as physical pressure—the pupae's being stepped on, heat from an animal lying on the pupae or increased carbon dioxide levels and vibrations—indicating that a suitable host is available.

Once hatched, the adult flea must feed within a few days. Once the adult flea finds a host, it will not leave voluntarily. It only becomes dislodged by grooming or the host animal's scratching. The adult flea will remain on the host for the duration of its life unless forcibly removed.

DID YOU KNOW?
Never mix flea control products without first consulting your veterinary surgeon. Some products can become toxic when combined with others and can cause serious or fatal consequences.

DID YOU KNOW?
Flea-killers are poisonous. You should not spray these toxic chemicals on areas of a dog's body that he licks, on his genitals or on his face. Flea killers taken internally are a better answer, but check with your vet in case internal therapy is not advised for your dog.

TREATING THE ENVIRONMENT AND THE DOG

Treating fleas should be a two-pronged attack. First, the environment needs to be treated; this includes carpets and furniture, especially the dog's bedding and areas underneath furniture. The environment should be treated with a household spray containing an Insect Growth Regulator (IGR) and an insecticide to kill the adult fleas. Most IGRs are effective against eggs and larvae; they actually mimic the fleas' own hormones and stop the eggs and larvae from developing into adult fleas. There are currently no treatments available to attack the pupa stage of the life cycle, so the adult insecticide is used to kill the newly hatched adult fleas before they find a host. Most IGRs are active for many months, whilst adult insecticides are only active for a few days.

When treating with a household spray, it is a good idea to vacuum before applying the

Opposite page: A scanning electron micrograph of a dog or cat flea, *Ctenocephalides*, magnified more than 100x. This image has been colorized for effect.

The Life Cycle of the Flea

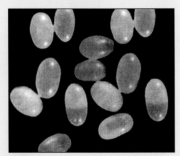

Eggs

Larva

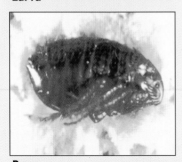

Pupa

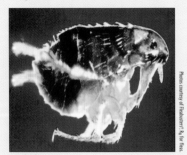

Adult

Photos courtesy of Fleabusters® R, for fleas.

Flea Control

IGR (INSECT GROWTH REGULATOR)

Two types of products should be used when treating fleas—a product to treat the pet and a product to treat the home. Adult fleas represent less than 1% of the flea population. The pre-adult fleas (eggs, larvae and pupae) represent more than 99% of the flea population and are found in the environment; it is in the case of pre-adult fleas that products containing an Insect Growth Regulator (IGR) should be used in the home.

IGRs are a new class of compounds used to prevent the development of insects. They do not kill the insect outright, but instead use the insect's biology against it to stop it from completing its growth. Products that contain methoprene are the world's first and leading IGRs. Used to control fleas and other insects, this type of IGR will stop flea larvae from developing and protect the house for up to seven months.

EN GARDE: CATCHING FLEAS OFF GUARD!

Consider the following ways to arm yourself against fleas:

• Add a small amount of pennyroyal or eucalyptus oil to your dog's bath. These natural remedies repel fleas.
• Supplement your dog's food with fresh garlic (minced or grated) and a hearty amount of brewer's yeast, both of which ward off fleas.
• Use a flea comb on your dog daily. Submerge fleas in a cup of bleach to kill them quickly.
• Confine the dog to only a few rooms to limit the spread of fleas in the home.
• Vacuum daily...and get all of the crevices! Dispose of the bag every few days until the problem is under control.
• Wash your dog's bedding daily. Cover cushions where your dog sleeps with towels, and wash the towels often.

product. This stimulates as many pupae as possible to hatch into adult fleas. The vacuum cleaner should also be treated with a flea treatment to prevent the eggs and larvae that have been hoovered into the vacuum bag from hatching.

The second stage of treatment is to apply an adult insecticide to the dog. Traditionally, this would be in the form of a collar or a spray, but more recent innovations include digestible insecticides that poison the fleas when they ingest the dog's blood. Alternatively, there are drops that, when placed on the back of the animal's neck, spread throughout the fur and skin to kill adult fleas.

PHOTO BY DWIGHT R KUHN

Dwight R Kuhn's magnificent action photo showing a flea jumping from a dog's back.

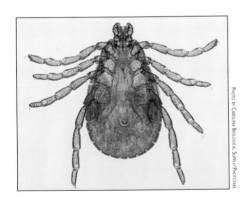

PHOTO BY CAROLINA BIOLOGICAL SUPPLY/PHOTOTAKE

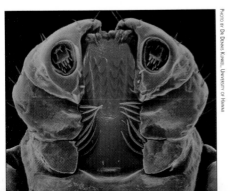

PHOTO BY DR DENNIS KUNKEL, UNIVERSITY OF HAWAII

TICKS AND MITES

Though not as common as fleas, ticks and mites are found all over the tropical and temperate world. They don't bite, like fleas; they harpoon. They dig their sharp proboscis (nose) into the dog's skin and drink the blood. Their only food and drink is dog's blood. Dogs can get Lyme disease, Rocky Mountain spotted fever (normally found in the US only), paralysis and many other diseases from ticks and mites. They may live where fleas are found and they like to hide in cracks or seams in walls wherever dogs live. They are controlled the same way fleas are controlled.

A brown dog tick, *Rhipicephalus sanguineus*, is an uncommon but annoying tick found on dogs.

The head of a dog tick, *Dermacentor variabilis*, enlarged and coloured for effect.

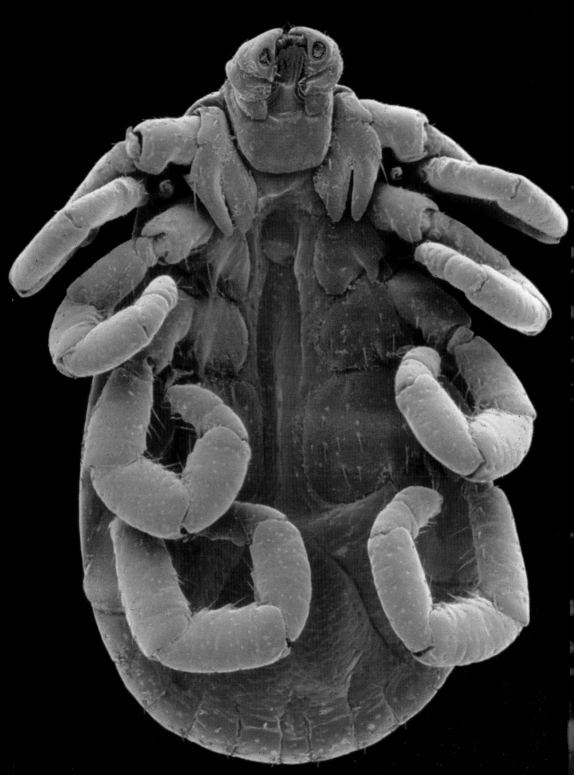

The dog tick, *Dermacentor variabilis*, may well be the most common dog tick in many geographical areas, especially those areas where the climate is hot and humid.

Most dog ticks have life expectancies of a week to six months, depending upon climatic conditions. They can neither jump nor fly, but they can crawl slowly and can range up to 5 metres (16 feet) to reach a sleeping or unsuspecting dog.

BEWARE THE DEER TICK

The great outdoors may be fun for your dog, but it also is a home to dangerous ticks. Deer ticks carry a bacterium known as *Borrelia burgdorferi* and are most active in the autumn and spring. When infections are caught early, penicillin and tetracycline are effective antibiotics, but if left untreated the bacteria may cause neurological, kidney and cardiac problems as well as long-term trouble with walking and painful joints.

Opposite page: The dog tick, *Dermacentor variabilis*, is probably the most common tick found on dogs. Look at the strength in its eight legs! No wonder it's hard to detach them.

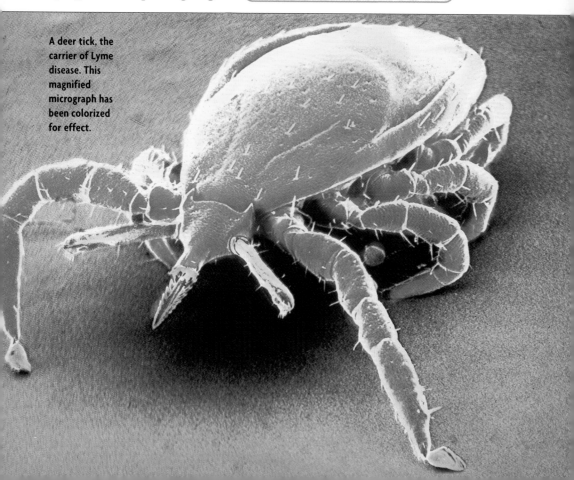

A deer tick, the carrier of Lyme disease. This magnified micrograph has been colorized for effect.

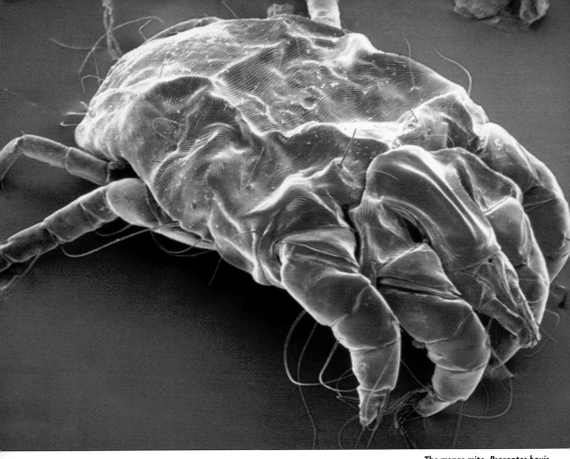

The mange mite, *Psoroptes bovis.*

Human lice look like dog lice; the two are closely related.

PHOTO BY DWIGHT R. KUHN

MANGE

Mites cause a skin irritation called mange. Some are contagious, like *Cheyletiella*, ear mites, scabies and chiggers. Mites that cause ear-mite infestations are usually controlled with Lindane, which can only be administered by a vet, followed by Tresaderm at home.

It is essential that your dog be treated for mange as quickly as possible because some forms of mange are transmissible to people.

INTERNAL PARASITES

Most animals—fishes, birds and mammals, including dogs and humans—have worms and other parasites that live inside their bodies. According to Dr Herbert R Axelrod, the fish pathologist, there are two kinds of parasites: dumb and smart. The smart parasites live in peaceful cooperation with their hosts (symbiosis), while the dumb parasites kill their host. Most of the worm infections are relatively easy to control. If they are not controlled they weaken the host dog to the point that other medical problems occur, but they are not dumb parasites.

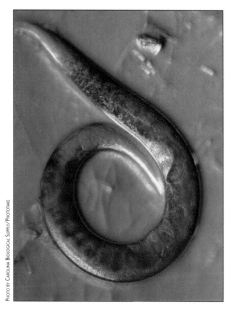

The roundworm, *Rhabditis*. The roundworm can infect both dogs and humans.

ROUNDWORMS

The roundworms that infect dogs are scientifically known as *Toxocara canis*. They live in the dog's intestines. The worms shed eggs continually. It has been estimated that a dog produces about 150 grammes of faeces every day. Each gramme of faeces averages 10,000–12,000 eggs of roundworms. There are no known areas in which dogs roam that do not contain roundworm eggs. The greatest danger of roundworms is that they infect people too! It is wise to have your dog tested regularly for roundworms.

Pigs also have roundworm infections that can be passed to humans and dogs. The typical roundworm parasite is called *Ascaris lumbricoides*.

ROUNDWORM

Average size dogs can pass 1,360,000 roundworm eggs every day.

For example, if there were only 1 million dogs in the world, the world would be saturated with 1,300 metric tonnes of dog faeces.

These faeces would contain 15,000,000,000 roundworm eggs.

It's known that 7–31% of home gardens and children's play boxes in the US contain roundworm eggs.

Flushing dog's faeces down the toilet is not a safe practice because the usual sewage treatments do not destroy roundworm eggs.

Infected puppies start shedding roundworm eggs at 3 weeks of age. They can be infected by their mother's milk.

DEWORMING

Ridding your puppy of worms is VERY IMPORTANT because certain worms that puppies carry, such as tapeworms and roundworms, can infect humans.

Breeders initiate a deworming programme at or about four weeks of age. The routine is repeated every two or three weeks until the puppy is three months old. The breeder from whom you obtained your puppy should provide you with the complete details of the deworming programme.

Your veterinary surgeon can prescribe and monitor the programme of deworming for you. The usual programme is treating the puppy every 15–20 days until the puppy is positively worm free.

It is advised that you only treat your puppy with drugs that are recommended professionally.

HOOKWORMS

The worm *Ancylostoma caninum* is commonly called the dog hookworm. It is dangerous to humans and cats. It also has teeth by which it attaches itself to the intestines of the dog. It changes the site of its attachment about six times a day and the dog loses blood from each detachment, possibly causing iron-deficiency anaemia. Hookworms are easily purged from the dog with many medications. Milbemycin oxime, which also serves as a heartworm preventative in Collies, can be used for this purpose.

In Britain the 'temperate climate' hookworm (*Uncinaria stenocephala*) is rarely found in pet or show dogs, but can occur in hunting packs, racing Greyhounds and sheepdogs because the worms can be prevalent wherever dogs are exercised regularly on grassland.

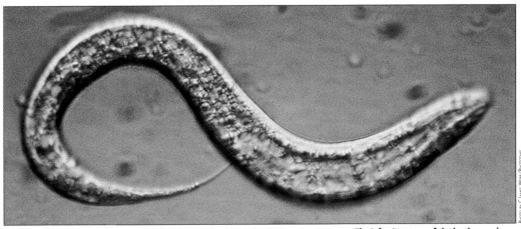

The infective stage of the hookworm larva.

PHOTO BY C JAMES WEBB/PHOTOTAKE

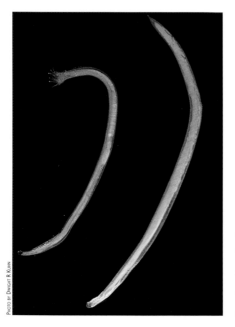

Photo by Dwight R Kuhn

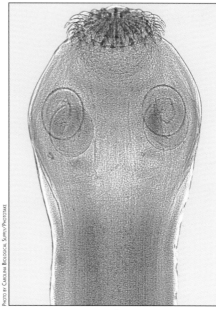

Photo by Carolina Biological Supply/Phototake

Left:
Male and female hookworms, *Ancylostoma caninum*, are uncommonly found in pet or show dogs in Britain. Hookworms may infect other dogs that have exposure to grasslands.

Right:
The head and rostellum (the round prominence on the scolex) of a tapeworm, which infects dogs and humans.

TAPEWORMS

There are many species of tapeworms. They are carried by fleas! The dog eats the flea and starts the tapeworm cycle. Humans can also be infected with tapeworms, so don't eat fleas! Fleas are so small that your dog could pass them onto your hands, your plate or your food and thus make it possible for you to ingest a flea which is carrying tapeworm eggs.

While tapeworm infection is not life threatening in dogs (smart parasite!), it can be the cause of a very serious liver disease for humans. About 50 percent of the humans infected with *Echinococcus multilocularis*, a type of tapeworm that causes alveolar hydatis, perish.

TAPEWORM

Humans, rats, squirrels, foxes, coyotes, wolves, mixed breeds of dogs and purebred dogs are all susceptible to tapeworm infection. Except in humans, tapeworms are usually not a fatal infection.

Infected individuals can harbour a thousand parasitic worms.

Tapeworms have two sexes—male and female (many other worms have only one sex—male and female in the same worm).

If dogs eat infected rats or mice, they get the tapeworm disease.

One month after attaching to a dog's intestine, the worm starts shedding eggs. These eggs are infective immediately.

Infective eggs can live for a few months without a host animal.

HEARTWORMS

Heartworms are thin, extended worms up to 30 cms (12 ins) long which live in a dog's heart and the major blood vessels surrounding it. Dogs may have up to 200 worms. Symptoms may be loss of energy, loss of appetite, coughing, the development of a pot belly and anaemia.

Heartworms are transmitted by mosquitoes. The mosquito drinks the blood of an infected dog and takes in larvae with the blood. The larvae, called microfilaria, develop within the body of the mosquito and are passed on to the next dog bitten after the larvae mature. It takes two to three weeks for the larvae to develop to the infective stage within the body of the mosquito. Dogs should be treated at about six weeks of age, and maintained on a prophylactic dose given monthly.

Blood testing for heartworms is not necessarily indicative of how seriously your dog is infected. This is a dangerous disease. Although heartworm is a problem for dogs in America, Australia, Asia and Central Europe, dogs in the United Kingdom are not currently affected by heartworm.

The heart of a dog infected with canine heartworm, *Dirofilaria immitis.*

PHOTO BY JAMES E HAYDEN, RPB./PHOTOTAKE

First Aid at a Glance

Burns
Place the affected area under cool water; use ice if only a small area is burnt.

Bee/Insect bites
Apply ice to relieve swelling; antihistamine dosed properly.

Animal bites
Clean any bleeding area; apply pressure until bleeding subsides; go to the vet.

Spider bites
Use cold compress and a pressurised pack to inhibit venom's spreading.

Antifreeze poisoning
Induce vomiting with hydrogen peroxide. Seek *immediate* veterinary help!

Fish hooks
Removal best handled by vet; hook must be cut in order to remove.

Snake bites
Pack ice around bite; contact vet quickly; identify snake for proper antivenin.

Car accident
Move dog from roadway with blanket; seek veterinary aid.

Shock
Calm the dog, keep him warm; seek immediate veterinary help.

Nosebleed
Apply cold compress to the nose; apply pressure to any visible abrasion.

Bleeding
Apply pressure above the area; treat wound by applying a cotton pack.

Heat stroke
Submerge dog in cold bath; cool down with fresh air and water; go to the vet.

Frostbite/Hypothermia
Warm the dog with a warm bath, electric blankets or hot water bottles.

Abrasions
Clean the wound and wash out thoroughly with fresh water; apply antiseptic.

 Remember: an injured dog may attempt to bite a helping hand from fear and confusion. Always muzzle the dog before trying to offer assistance.

INDEX

*Page numbers in **boldface** indicate illustrations.*

My Welsh Springer Spaniel

PUT YOUR PUPPY'S FIRST PICTURE HERE

Dog's Name _____

Date _____ Photographer _____